C0-AYH-177

Series/Number 06-011

Corporatism and Public Policy in Authoritarian Portugal

PHILIPPE C. SCHMITTER
University of Chicago/
University of Geneva

SAGE Publications/London/Beverly Hills

For information address:

SAGE PUBLICATIONS, Ltd.,
St. George's House/44 Hatton Garden
London EC1N 8ER

SAGE PUBLICATIONS, INC.
275 South Beverly Drive
Beverly Hills, California 90212

International Standard Book Number 0-8039-9914-3

Library of Congress Catalogue Card No. L.C. 75-5279

FIRST PRINTING

Printed by Wells & Blackwell Ltd., Loughborough, Leics.

CONTENTS

List of Tables

List of Figures

Corporatism and Public Policy in Authoritarian Portugal

PHILIPPE C. SCHMITTER

> *The Twentieth Century will be the century of corporatism just as the Nineteenth was the century of liberalism. . .*
>
> – M. Manoïlesco

After its brief haunting of the European scene in the 1920s and 1930s, Manoïlesco's spectre seemed to have permanently retired to the Museum of Political Bric-à-Brac along with divine right monarchy, democracy by lot and (hopefully) the *Führerprinzip*. Corporatism or corporativism was so closely linked in the popular lexicon with Fascism that as a concept the former could hardly have expected to survive the collapse and disgrace of the latter.

One polity, however, stood alone in proudly proclaiming itself 'a corporative state'. That was Portugal. Given its protracted experience with this system of interest representation and political control, the elaborateness of the institutional structures which were created under its aegis and the explicitness of the ideological statements extolling its virtues, Portugal presented an excellent and virtually unparalleled opportunity for exploring the nature and consequences of modern or neo-corporatism. Perhaps equally important were the absence of an exhaustive civil war and neutrality in World War II. Portugal, one could argue, was for a long time a sort of actualized ideal type relatively uncontaminated by the germs of international strife (thanks to deliberate isolation), exposure to subversive ideologies (thanks to protracted censorship and linguistic marginality), massive upheavals in occupational structure or urban-rural balance (thanks

I would like to thank the Social Science Research Council for a post-doctoral grant which enabled me to travel to Portugal in the summer of 1971 and the Council on Foreign Relations for support during 1973/74 which has permitted me to revise and extend my original draft. Lack of space and a prudent desire not to associate them with the ideas and interpretation expressed in this essay preclude my thanking personally the many Portuguese scholars and interest group leaders who responded so patiently and helpfully to my requests for information.

to relative economic and social stagnation), or even, crises of political succession (thanks to Salazar's extraordinary personal longevity). Better than any other contemporary setting, Portugal afforded us the opportunity to analyze institutionalized authoritarian rule with corporatism as one of its structural cornerstones (see also Linz, 1970: 251-283; Schmitter, 1971: 366-394).

Since these conditions of virtual laboratory-like control were fast disappearing under the combined effects of massive emigration, protracted international guerrilla campaigns in Africa, modest economic progress and pervasive tourism, one might even argue that the study of contemporary Portugal commanded a certain priority or urgency. It also presented us with a challenging case study of emergent political change. Could this, so far ultra-stable form of authoritarian rule adapt to these emergent multiple pressures without transforming itself into a different form of political domination (but see Anderson, 1970)?

The answer to this query came far sooner than this author imagined. On 25 April 1974 the Caetano regime was overthrown by a *coup d'état* led by junior officers of the armed forces. In a very short time and virtually without resistance, the corporatist structures described and analyzed in this essay were dismantled. They have since been largely replaced by a burgeoning number of voluntary pluralistic associations. While this essay may contribute little to a specific understanding of why and when the *coup* occurred, I believe it does help explain why the state corporatist structures, indeed the authoritarian regime itself proved to be so vulnerable and impotent.

Therefore, I have changed very little from earlier drafts of this essay, except to put much of it in the appropriate past tense. The field research upon which it is based was conducted in the summer of 1971. The present version of the essay was completed in the summer of 1973. I have merely added a short epilogue to bring it up to date.

Given a unique and apparently anachronistic setting, one had a tendency when analyzing Portugal to see oneself as a sort of 'political paleontologist,' the student of a quaint institutional fossil which somehow survived the catastrophes which befell its cohorts of the 1920s and 1930s. Whatever one discovered in terms of patterned relationships or consequences would seem of primary utility for understanding the past and of very dubious relevance for the future. I admit to having approached Portugal with that sort of 'antiquarian' perspective in view.

One quickly discovered that Portuguese establishment statesmen, ideologues and propagandists had no such view of their own corporatist institutions. Far from considering them historical atavisms, they argued with abundant illustrations that the rest of postwar Europe has tended to practise a disguised form of corporatism and that this emergent pattern of interest representation was converging with that practised by Portugal since the early 1930s. While occasionally conceding the need to reform some of their more restrictive practices in order to accommodate to the requirements of a more open and expansive economy, they were not convinced that their system was all that different from those of developed European countries and were very convinced that it was becoming steadily less so (see Nunes, 1954; Pinto, 1955; Cardoso, 1958).

Partially and for rather different reasons and values I too came to regard Portugal as something of a prototype. It was almost as if Portugal, treading water and/or swimming against the tide for forty years or so, gradually found that the earlier developing, liberal democracies which swam or drifted with the predominant historical currents had been swept in a giant circle. Increasingly, they seemed to be bobbing up alongside this isolated, idiosyncratic and 'backward' country. Of course, having taken a different route to structurally similar decisional and representational practices, relations of power and influence were likely to be different, even inverted, but the formal institutional outcome was strikingly convergent.

Naturally, these modern democratic polities do not openly proclaim themselves corporatist, although they have occasionally been so baptized by irreverent intellectual observers.[1] Why should they openly embrace such a historically discredited ideology and practice? Especially when there has been no manifest collapse of the previous liberal-pluralist-competitive order and, hence, no need to rationalize, justify, extoll or otherwise account for such a subtle transformation (Harris, 1972: 72-73).[2]

All this is not to say that the study of Portugal converted me from paleontologist to futurist; that, inverting Marx, I was prepared to argue that "the lesser developed industrial nation only shows to the more developed the image of its own future", but it is intended to suggest that in a circular and paradoxical universe where the course of political development is not so naturally cumulative, irreversible and unilinear, and where our ability to conceptualize change is often obfuscated by established linguistic convention, it becomes difficult to discern what constitutes progress and regress (Schmitter, 1972a: 83-108).

What was particularly striking about Portugal was the architectonic effort of a narrow élite, even of a single man, who quite explicitly set out to create, from above and in anticipation, institutions of limited representation, participation and influence and of comprehensive administrative control which would insulate that society and state from "subversion" by either liberalism or socialism, at the same time laying the basis for a capitalist economic system in the absence of a vigorous and autonomous national capitalist class. Development without change; participation without freedom; capitalism without capitalists.

This essay is an attempt to describe how this was initiated in the 1930s, to analyze how this authoritarian response to modernization evolved and persisted and finally to assess what have been its consequences for the welfare, freedom and security of the Portuguese people. Has this type of regime had a plausible and measurable impact on policy outputs and outcomes? For this latter purpose, rather than indulge in counter-factual speculation about the probable policy impact of Portugal having sustained more open and competitive political instutions, I will rely on matched comparisons with Ireland and Greece. These countries had a parametric configuration in economy, society and culture strikingly similar to that of Portugal in 1925-30. By comparing over time their relative policy performances, we can perhaps obtain a more empirically grounded estimate of what have been the costs and benefits of corporatist representation and authoritarian rule for the Portuguese people.

THE CONCEPT OF CORPORATISM

Corporatism is a term, like liberalism or socialism, which is difficult to use in analytical discourse. Not only have a wide variety of ideologues identified themselves as Corporatists with a capital 'C', but an even wider variety of actors have advocated or practised it under obfuscatory labels. Its historic but partly accidental association with Fascism has made it a handy epithet to be tossed at all interest group systems of which one does not approve. Although there has been a resurgence recently of 'corporatist' name-calling (often along with 'fascist'), the concept can be stripped of at least part of its normal language meaning and used in a non-polemic sense to refer to a system of interest representation whose constituent structures and interdependent relations differ markedly, if not diametrically, from those of pluralism.

The following admittedly overelaborated and multifaceted definition would seem to capture the distinctive features of modern corporatism as an ideal-type, i.e. as a heuristic, logico-analytical construct of theoretically interrelated components.

> Corporatism can be defined as a system of interest representation in which the constituent units are organized into a limited number of singular, compulsory,

> non-competitive, hierarchically-ordered and functionally differentiated categories, recognized or licensed (if not created) by the state and granted a deliberate representational monopoly within their respective categories in exchange for observing certain controls on their selection of leaders and articulation of demands and supports.

Pluralism, while it shares much in common with corporatism, e.g. the group-centered view of the political process, the ineluctably modern drive of associability, the socialization effect of participation in formal secondary structures, differs from it markedly in ideal-typical terms.

> Pluralism is a system of interest representation in which the constituent units are organized into an unspecified number of multiple, voluntary, competitive, non-hierarchically ordered and self-determined (as to type or scope of interest) categories not specially licensed, subsidized, created or otherwise controlled by the State and not exercising a monopoly of representational activity within their respective categories.

Of course, no historically extant polity has conformed completely to either ideal-type. All are hybrid to a degree. Portugal's peculiarity lay in the fact that it more manifestly approached the corporatist model than any other polity, present or past. The fact that none of the so-called or self-proclaimed democratic polities comes as close to impersonating the ideal pluralist model should give us pause. Could it be that corporatism is a more natural (or at least more frequent) outcome of structural and attitudinal differentiation than pluralism? [3]

Our use of the concept, corporatism, should not be confounded with or treated as identical to that used by any one of the variety of theorists/ideologues/activists who have advocated it (*avant, après ou pendant la lettre*). One of the most fascinating and confusing aspects of corporatism as an ideology is the way in which actors with widely divergent motives, interests and reasons have converged upon it. There are 'leftist' corporatists as well as 'rightist' ones; 'nationalist' as well as 'internationalist' ones, 'traditionalists' as well as 'modernists', etc. Crudely speaking, four schools of corporatist thought can be distinguished: (1) A social christian, ethically traditionalist one exemplified by such thinkers as Albert de Mun, and the Marquis de la Tour de Pin, culminating in *Rerum Novarum* of Leo XIII and *Quadrasgesimo Anno* of Pio XI (Azpaizu, 1951; Elbow, 1953); (2) An authoritarian, bureaucratic nationalist and secular modernizing form whose central theorist is Mihaïl Manoïlesco and which includes most of the Italian corporatist ideologues: Ugo Spirito, Giuseppe Bottai, Guido Bortolotto, as well as Othmar Spann in Austria (Manoïlesco, 1934; Pirou, 1938 & 1939); (3) A radical (in the French party sense), parliamentary, bourgeois solidarist tradition as exemplified by such thinkers as Léon Bougeois, Charles Gide, Emile Boutroux and Emile Durkheim;[4] (4) finally, a leftist, socialist, syndicalist line of thought which originates with Saint-Simon (probably the first modern corporatist) and evolves into such diverse currents as George Sorel, Enrico Corradini, Edmondo Rossini, Gregor Strasser, Henri de Man, Marcel Déat, Oswald Mosley, the Guild Socialists and, Trotsky would have us believe, Joseph Stalin.[5]

All of these, and the list is by no means complete,[6] converged upon the advocacy of an institutional relationship between the system of authoritative decision-making and that of interest aggregation similar to that defined above as generically corporatist, although they conceived of this arrangement as involving radically different arrangements of power and influence, as benefiting quite distinct social classes, and as promoting diametrically opposite public policies.

THE PRACTICE OF CORPORATISM IN PORTUGAL

Because of a lack of equilibrium in the human spirit, order is not spontaneous; someone must command for the benefit of all.

– O. Salazar

By ideological pedigree, Portuguese corporatism was manifestly and insistently derived from the Social Christian, ethically reactionary tradition. By governmental practice, it more closely approximated to the type advocated by the authoritarian, bureaucratic, nationalist school. In the vocabulary of Manoïlesco, it may have been *intégral* in its attempt to cover virtually all spheres of interest articulation, but, as we shall see, it was clearly *impur* in its consistent subordination of representational units to the imperative command of a highly centralized administrative apparatus and in its persistent marginality with regard to the policy-making process.

On one point, most schools of corporatism agree. A system of interest representation which is unitary, non-competitive and hierarchically-structured will not emerge naturally, of its own accord. The state must intervene creatively (and restrictively) to make it so. Free, spontaneous (hence, chaotic and conflictful) associability must be controlled and channelled by means of what one of my students aptly termed an enforced 'genetic code' of legitimate group formation (Bachelor, 1973).

Corporatists, then, tend to be 'political architects'. They discourse learnedly, lengthily and heatedly over what should be the proper 'functions' around which corporations will be formed; the desirable levels at which subgroups should be federated or combined; the best point at which to differentiate, if at all, workers' and employers' associations; the appropriate degree of subordination to state control, etc. In most cases, very elaborate, *a priori* schemes are set forth outlining detailed legal categories for the *enquadramento* (in Portuguese, literally, 'the framing') of all societal interests. Not only is corporatism to be imposed from above, but its structure should be deduced from general theoretical principles.

The practice of corporatist regimes such as Italy (Sarti, 1971) and Brazil (Schmitter, 1971: ch. V) followed such formalistic lines. Even if subsequent research has revealed these impressive, uniformly symmetric national structures to have been mere façades shot through with expedient, pragmatic exemptions and special arrangements; both Mussolini and Vargas did attempt to lay out a single, balanced, functionally specified organization-chart covering all existing and potential categories of economic interest.

What is particularly striking about Portugal in the early 1930s is that it did not begin with such a singular, grandiose, formalistic and comprehensive scheme. Although Salazar himself definitely had an architectonic vision of an 'integral' corporatist order,[7] he (or better his designated agents such as Pedro Teotónio Pereira [1937]), and João Pinto de Costa Leite (Lumbrales) (1936), proceeded very cautiously and incrementally to assemble this system of representation: piece-by-piece, sector-by-sector, level-by-level. In fact so cautiously did they proceed that Portuguese corporatism operated for twenty-five years without *corporações,* that is without the nominal capstones of its organizational structure! These were not created until after 1956 and some never functioned regularly.

Perhaps more than other corporatisms, the Portuguese variant must be understood historically, as the product of a continuous and protracted political process. The extraordinary complexity of its eventual configuration was baffling and quite misleading unless related to the timing, sequence and rates of change which marked its institutional evolution. This is *not* to say that Portuguese corporatism did not have some of the same façade-like structural properties of the *de toutes pièces* Italian and Brazilian systems, or to claim that it was an authentic and 'organic' outcome of Portuguese societal development – not at all – but it was a more realistic product of experimentation and interaction, of accommodation to prior associational practice, changing international contexts and internal social and economic change than other corporatist systems.

ASSOCIABILITY IN PORTUGAL BEFORE THE 'NEW STATE'

The pattern of associability in Portugal prior to 1930-33 did not differ markedly from that followed earlier by other European nations. The exception might be the medieval period when Portugal witnessed an unusually vigorous development of 'corporations of arts and offices' (guilds) in virtually all its urban centers. The twelve most important of these were grouped, with two representatives apiece, into 'Houses of the Twenty-Four'. These in turn provided a powerful basis for municipal, political and even juridical autonomy. To the extent that Portugal can lay claim to a tradition of pluralist decentralization, it lies in these associations of guilds with their popularly-elected 'Judges of the People'.[8]

The historical origins of Portuguese medieval corporatism, then, were virtually concomitant with the very founding of the dynastic state by Mestre de Aviz in 1384. The political development of the latter, however, easily displaced the former. Already weakened by the absolutist, physiocratic reforms of the Marquês de Pombal in 1761, the *Casas dos Vinte e Quatro*, their component guilds, the office of 'Judges of the People' and all corporatist privileges were swept aside by the liberal reforms of 1834. These also expressly prohibited the formation of associations for defence of working class interests. In 1864 workers were granted the right to establish 'mutual aid societies' and finally in 1891 an omnibus 'Law of Class Associations' was decreed, recognizing all forms of associability, but subjecting its products to prior governmental approval, placing restrictions on the political scope of their activity and controlling the formation of regional or national 'Unions' of associations. Apparently, the restrictive portions of this law 'became a mere formality that did not constitute an authentic preventive control, only a mere register or administrative *cadastre*'.[9] In 1924, the right to form federations or national unions was granted. Previously, in 1910 the right to strike had been conceded by the newly incumbent Republic.

Associational practice only partially reflected these changing legal parameters. The guilds were apparently moribund before their formal dissolution. No present day Portuguese interest group can (nor does) claim a direct line of descendance from these *corporações de artes e ofícios.* The very year of the liberal constitutional reforms, 1834, saw the founding of the Associaçao Mercentil Lisbonense, later and currently called the Associação Comercial de Lisboa. The Associação Comercial do Porto was established in 1834. Others followed in Figueira da Foz and Setúbal (da Fonseca, 1934).

The first entity representing industrial employer interests, the Associação Industrial Portuense, was founded in 1849 in Porto and eleven years later the industrialists of Lisbon created the Associação Promotora de Indústria Fabril which subsequently became the present day Associação Industrial Portuguesa. In that same year (1860) agricultural interests received a charter for their Royal Central Association of Portuguese Agriculture.

The working classes responded even more vigorously to this period of relatively free, voluntary associability, despite 'anti-subversive' repressive measures (Junior, 1964; Vieira, 1950 and 1970; Silva, 1971; Pacheco, 1971). The first 'proletarian' (artisanal would be more accurately descriptive) group, the Associação dos Artistas Lisbonenses, was founded in 1839. A second spurt of organization occurred in the 1850s, but the first major organization for working class defence, the Associação Protectora do Trabalho Nacional, did not emerge until 1871. Anarchism quickly gained a strong following among artisans and the dispute between them and the socialists, along with differences between the working classes of Lisbon and Porto, prevented the formation of viable national entities. Various national 'congresses' and 'meetings' were held in the 1890s and 1900s, but formal 'syndical unity' was only attained (União Operária Nacional) after the proclamation of the Republic. Portuguese entry into World War I had an enormous impact on working class militancy. The UON was transformed into an augmented Conferação General do Trabalho (CGT) and the strike rate soared to levels unparalleled in previous Portuguese history, perhaps the highest in Europe for that period. Intensive agitation carried over into the interwar period, fed by competition between communist, socialist and anarchist factions.

TABLE 1: STRIKES IN PORTUGAL: 1852-1925

	1852-59	1860-69	1870-79	1880-89	1890-99	1900-09	1910-19	1920-25
Number of Strikes	2	0	15	12	38	91	391	127

Source: Costa Junior, 1964: 59-113.

This burgeoning rate of association formation and activity was not confined to the urban proletariat. Costa Junior reports that in 1912 a Congress of Rural Syndicates was held with 39 organizations attending, claiming a total membership of 12,600. Centered in the southern, latifundista region of the country, this autonomous movement alone conducted 70 strikes (Cutileiro, 1971: 83-87 and 216-227).

As this brief account abundantly testifies, the corporatists in the early 1930s were not faced with an associational vacuum. Differentiated sectors and relatively cohesive social classes had forged organizational instruments for the articulation and defense of their interests with little support or subsidization from the state and often in the face of its strong opposition. The *Annuario Estatistico* of 1921 contained some (admittedly incomplete) data on the number and memberships of various types of associations (see Table 2). Less complete information in the 1923-24 *Annuario* showed a marked rise in the total number of 'class associations', an increase from 730 to 853 in only two years. When the corporatists in 1934 checked the files on registered class associations, they found 1,076 effectively functioning (as Corporações na Economià Nacional, 1971: 39). Granted that many of those may have had a rather irregular institutional existence,

TABLE 2: NUMBER AND MEMBERSHIP IN REPRESENTATION ASSOCIATIONS – 1921

	Number of Groups	Number of Members
1. Associaçoes de Classe (includes employers, workers, and a few mixed entities)		
a. Industry	425	46,277
b. Commerce, services and transport	219	39,127
c. Agriculture, fishing	86	11,018
Total	730	96,422
2. Associaçoes de Socorros Mútuos (Mutual aid societies, mostly of urban workers and artisans)	668	?
3. Sindicatos Agrícolas (Rural workers syndicates)	276	29,493

Source: República Portuguesa.

that their membership figures might have been grossly inflated, that their coverage of interests and issues might have been a good deal less than their formal titles suggested; nevertheless, one simply cannot accept the view, propounded by corporatist ideologues, that pre-Estado Novo Portugal was an "invertebrate" associational wasteland, populated only by scattered and ephemeral bands of ultraradical extremists. Rather, the society seems to have cultivated its 'art of association' to a degree commensurate with its level of economic development and social mobilization.[10] In fact, this art was sufficiently developed on the part of subordinate classes and sectors to pose a genuine threat, not only to the survival of a weak, petit bourgeois, democratic regime, but to the successful implantation of a new authoritarian bureaucratic order.

THE IMPLANTATION OF CORPORATIST REPRESENTATION

> *The Portuguese State is a unitary and corporative Republic.* – Art. 5, The Portuguese Constitution (1933)

When Salazar announced his plan to replace the interim dictatorial military regime (1926-33) with an *Estado Novo* free from the disorders of 'individualism', 'socialism', 'parliamentarism' and 'partisan spirit', corporation was advanced as one of its 'fundamental principles'.[11] Its inclusion could hardly have come as a surprise to anyone. Not only had Salazar himself been active in a Catholic faction at the University of Coimbra, the Centro Academico de Democracia Crista (CADC), which strongly advocated such a policy along lines inspired by Albert de Mun, Marquis de la Tour du Pin and *Rerum Novarum,* but other individuals and groups had long been actively promoting corporatist 'solutions'. Throughout the nineteenth century there was an uninterrupted series of corporatist academics and intellectuals, of vaguely Saint-Simonist and positivist inspiration (Teixeira, 1961: 39-49). Much more important was the founding of a nationalist movement, *Integralismo Lusitano* (1914), of Maurrassien inspiration whose corporatism was more militantly authoritarian and, at least verbally, anti-capitalist.[12] Mussolini's *Carta del Lavoro* was, of course, still a fresh and apparently budding success in the opinion of many.[13] Actually, Portugal had already attempted during the very brief, 'populist' reign of Sidónio Pais (1917-18) some corporatist-type experiments, long before the better known 'innovations' of Primo de Rivera, Mussolini and Dolfuss (Martins, 1968: 309). In short, not only was corporatism very much a part of the general political ambience of Europe in the early 1930s, it also had multiple and specific historical and ideological roots in Portugal itself.[14]

From 1922-33 Salazar had more or less accomplished his short-term primary objective, the balancing of the governmental budget, thereby arresting the depreciation of the Portuguese currency and domestic inflation.[15] As he turned to his more long-range political objective, the establishment of a stable, civilian authoritarian regime,[16] the deliberate and forceful corporatization of the interest group system was aimed at accomplishing two immediate purposes.

First and most obviously, the corporatization of the working class was designed, not simply to deprive this class of the instruments of collective struggle which it had forged since the 1840s (the activities of these organizations had been repressed severely since 1927), but to provide governmental authorities with a complex network of new institutions to capture information on worker dissatisfaction, channel selective welfare benefits to 'worthy' sectors, coopt emergent and potentially challenging leaders, restrict wages and salaries in the name of austerity and balance and, most of all, occupy a certain 'organizational space', thereby preventing the eventual emergence of competing representative associations. The rapidity and subsequent consistency with which this was accomplished was extraordinary.

On the same day (23 September 1933), the Statute of National Labor (ETN) and Decree-Law No. 23050 were promulgated. The former outlined in rather general terms what were henceforth to be the rules of interest representation and conflict (defense of private property, class harmony, state recognition of associations and control over their activities, prohibition of strikes and lockouts, establishment of labor courts); the latter set out in great detail the conditions under which urban workers' and employers' organizations (*Sindicatos Nacionais*), could form and operate (singular recognition per category, confinement to the district level, strict control over formation of territorial federations or 'intersectorial unions', government approval of all candidates for syndical office, ample and ambiguous grounds for governmental intervention and/or dissolution of syndicates, prohibition on political activity and on internation affiliation, etc.).[17] Civil servants and government employers at whatever level were denied the right to form syndicates, but the initiative in forming those permitted was left formally to private individuals. Also, membership was left voluntary, although once recognized a syndicate officially represents the interests of all workers in the designated category and financial contributions to its coffers can become mandatory.

TABLE 3: NUMERICAL PROLIFERATION OF WORKERS' SYNDICATES: 1935-65

Urban Employees' and Workers' Organization (Sindicatos Nacionais)	1935		1940		1945		1950		1955		1960		1965	
	N	%	N	%	N	%	N	%	N	%	N	%	N	%
1. Economic Sector														
Industry	83	(43.5)	135	(48.9)	159	(51.6)	172	(55.1)	170	(54.3)	172	(53.3)	173	(53.4)
Transport and Communications	45	(23.6)	65	(23.6)	64	(20.8)	59	(18.9)	62	(19.8)	64	(19.8)	62	(19.1)
Commerce and Services	48	(25.1)	55	(19.9)	64	(20.8)	60	(19.2)	62	(19.8)	66	(20.4)	68	(21.0)
Liberal Professional	15	(7.9)	21	(7.6)	21	(6.8)	21	(6.7)	19	(6.0)	21	(6.5)	21	(6.5)
2. Location														
Lisbon	62	(32.5)	82	(29.7)	90	(29.2)	90	(28.8)	87	(27.8)	85	(26.3)	87	(26.8)
Porto	38	(19.9)	55	(19.9)	55	(17.9)	53	(17.0)	54	(17.3)	55	(17.0)	54	(16.7)
Rest of Country	91	(47.6)	139	(50.4)	163	(52.9)	169	(54.2)	171	(54.6)	183	(56.7)	185	(57.1)
3. Scope														
National	17	(8.9)	28	(10.1)	32	(10.4)	35	(11.2)	33	(10.5)	33	(10.2)	32	(9.9)
Inter-district	5	(2.6)	36	(13.0)	86	(27.9)	80	(25.6)	84	(26.8)	88	(27.2)	96	(29.6)
District Only	169	(88.5)	212	(76.9)	190	(61.7)	197	(63.1)	196	(62.6)	202	(62.5)	196	(60.5)
4. Member Dues														
Obligatory	?		?		264	(85.7)	278	(89.1)	283	(90.4)	302	(93.5)	?	
Voluntary	?		?		44	(14.3)	34	(10.9)	30	(9.6)	17	(5.3)	?	
TOTAL	191		276		308		312		313		323		324	

As Table 3 testifies, the proliferation of urban workers' syndicates advanced at a furious rate. Within two years of its promulgation, Decree Law 23050 had spawned 191 entities.[18] By 1945, the number reached 308. In the ensuing twenty years the total has increased by only 16! In short, the Portuguese corporatist system for urban workers was put together in about ten years and has hardly changed in numerical terms since. Also striking is its structural consistency (petrification if you prefer) revealed by the sectoral and geographical breakdowns. There is some indication of an initial concentration of effort on the service sector (commerce, transport and communications), but by 1945 52 per cent of all *Sindicatos* were industrial – a proportion which hardly changed in the subsequent years. Lisbon and Porto were the headquarters for 32 per cent and 20 per cent of the syndicates formed before 1935, and this had dropped only slightly to 27 per cent and 16 per cent respectively by 1965.

The other two breakdowns show a bit more evidence of insitutional change. As mentioned, Decree No. 23050 was designed to fragment workers' organizations and confine them to the smallest feasible administrative unit, the *districto.* The only sectors permitted national coverage were the liberal professional 'Orders' of physicians, lawyers, architects, etc. and some categories of merchant marine officers and seamen. Gradually, however, the number of syndicates covering more than one district (usually only two) rose, apparently because it proved financially difficult to support such tiny aggregates of interest.[19] The incomplete data in section 4 of Table 3 about whether or not membership dues were compulsory indicate a clear trend toward the state exercising its option to extend mandatory financial contribution to cover non-members. Needless to say, this was used on a discretionary basis to reward compliant syndicates and punish recalcitrant ones.

Yet another decree (No. 23051) promulgated on that fateful 23 September 1933, initiated the corporatization of rural workers. It ordered the creation in every rural *frequesia* (an administrative unit even smaller than the *districto,* roughly equivalent to a French *commune*) of a *Casa do Povo* or House of the People. Unlike the urban National Syndicates, these *Casas* were constituted as 'mixed entities' with a joint membership of rural workers and rural landowners. Their decreed internal structure was rigged in such a way as to guarantee that 'protecting members', i.e. landlords, would control the decision process (Lucena, 1971: Vol. 1, 129; Lopez-Cardoso, 1968: 761-780). Furthermore, the *Casas* were explicitly denied any representative function (and therefore, ofter referred to as *pre*-syndical bodies). Their designated role was to provide some marginal welfare and relief services, to make available educational and cultural facilities and to encourage various community improvements. To these ends, they were very modestly financed by an obligatory tax on landowners and semi-voluntary (involuntary after 1941) dues from rural workers. While in some regions of the country, i.e. the North, this lack of class differentiation in the composition of the *Casas* could have been defended sociologically on the grounds that the proliferation of *minifundistas* was so great and their resources so small and precarious that the distinction between property-owner and worker was difficult to make and subject to continuous variation, the same case could hardly be made for the latifundista South where the mixed but rigid structure of the *Casas* made them a blatant instrument of class domination. Later, when rural landowners' guilds (*Grémios da Lavoura*) were established and *Casas do Povo* formally granted certain representational functions, landowners 'representing' rural workers were called on to bargain with landowners representing landowners.[20]

Table 4 shows that the pattern of *Casa* formation resembled that of urban *Sindicatos.* A very large number were created immediately after the decree. By 1945 there were 506 of them in metropolitan Portugal. Here, however, contrary to the former case there is evidence of numerical growth and extension of territorial coverage in the more recent period, after some fifteen years of postwar stagnation. Also interesting is the marked shift in the geographical locus of association activity. Initially, the network was centered on the South and Central regions (incidentally, the regions of the greatest voluntary organization in the Republican period and those of greatest concentration of landholdings). Only gradually has it been extended northward and inland to regions of more intensive cultivation and dispersed ownership.

The evidence so far suggests that Portuguese corporatism, as least in its initial phase, was not only a device for consolidating an authoritarian political system but was also an instrument of class rule. It appeared aimed at disarming and rendering dependent upon state-sponsored paternalism those groups whose articulated demands might have hindered the accumulation of national entrepreneurial capital *and* hampered the consolidation of the political hegemony of a national bougeoisie.

This, however, is only part of the picture. For, on that very same fateful 23 September, yet another decree was promulgated initiating the corporatism of propertied interests into 'compulsory *Grémios*' or guilds (Decree No. 23049). According to it, the State at its initiative could command the creation of employer guilds in whatever industrial, commercial or agricultural sector; require all those operating in that sector to join and contribute; exercise comprehensive control over their internal

TABLE 4. NUMERICAL PROLIFERATION OF CASÁS DO POVO: 1935-65

	1935		1940		1945		1950		1955		1960		1965	
		%		%		%		%		%		%		%
I. CASAS DO POVO														
North	34	(24.1)	100	(31.3)	206	(40.7)	206	(41.4)	209	(40.8)	230	(40.5)	256	(41.0)
Interior	34	(24.1)	83	(26.0)	109	(21.5)	105	(21.0)	109	(21.3)	117	(20.6)	140	(22.4)
Center	34	(24.1)	49	(15.4)	65	(12.8)	57	(11.4)	61	(11.9)	77	(13.6)	82	(13.1)
South	38	(27.0)	71	(22.3)	111	(21.9)	114	(22.9)	15	(22.5)	24	(21.8)	127	(20.3)
Islands	1	(?)	16	(5.0)	15	(3.0)	16	(3.2)	18	(3.5)	20	(3.5)	20	(3.2)
TOTAL	141		319		506		498		512		568		625	

decisional process;[21] and render decisions of the *Grémio* legally binding on all members. On paper, state controls over this form of employer associability are even stricter than those over worker syndicates. At least, the latter could vote with their feet when faced with such imposed contributions – and did.

The regime, in actual practice, made rather sparing use of Decree No. 23049. By 1954 only 53 of 495 employer *Grémios* were obligatory, but this number had increased to 91 of 559 by 1967. Initially, their purpose was fairly clear – to organize from above and regulate the production and distribution of certain commodities which were essential to Portugal's foreign trade (wine, canned fish, fruit, wool, lumber) or national consumption (codfish, wheat, rice, commercialization of certain imports, flour milling and bread). Although they were explained as exceptional, 'heroic' measures taken in response to the collapse of world markets in the Depression and the immediate need for autarkic production (Pereira, 1937: 72-73), these compulsory guilds have not been subsequently disbanded. In fact, they increased, particularly in the post World War II period.

There exists evidence in the form of disgruntled statements by the original architects of corporatism that propertied groups so benefited, did not exactly appreciate the favor of having their prices, quotas, credits, distribution of subsidies, conditions of operation, fines, etc., regimented by *their* representative associations, to say nothing of heavy involuntary dues and taxes (Pereira, 1937: 187-189, 192; Caetano, no date: 126-127). Although it is not clear what the longer term incidence effects of such extensive administrative controls have been upon the distribution of benefits, the emergent authoritarian regime did 'take on' and subordinate organizationally some of the most politically influential sectors of the Portuguese economy, e.g. production and commercialization of wine and the milling of grain. On paper, at least, the detailed administrative regulations concerning these commodities and sectors were aimed at ensuring the marketing of goods for smaller producers and at reducing excess capacity among larger firms. They certainly reduced insecurity from competition and prevented displacement by new, more efficient, producers. Presumably they did so by passing on the costs to consumers, national and international. In any case, this attempt to corporatize the economy simultaneously with the system of interest representation seems to have failed. Already by 1936, the state was moving extensively into the direct regulation of economic activity through the creation of para-ministerial administrative bodies, e.g. the National Board for Cork, The Regulatory Commission for Codfish, The Institute for Douro Wine, the House of Port Wine, etc., rather than extending the coverage of obligatory *Grémios.*[22]

Actually, the regime had already left a compensatory loophole in the original 1933 decree, a provision which recognized and tolerated the continued existence of 'class associations' already in existence. While it completely obliterated all previous workers' organizations, there is no evidence that any of the 285 existing employers' association were forcibly closed – although many subsequently dissolved themselves voluntarily. The Industrial Associations in Lisbon and Porto and the various Chambers of Commerce remained in existence and continued to articulate their respective class and sector interests. The regime found it prudent to work with (and occasionally around) these traditional patronal entities. On the employer side, therefore, the system was never *exclusively* corporatist.[23]

One year after the first *Grémio* decree, the regime opened yet another range of associational opportunities to employers. According to Decree No. 24715 they could create, at their initiative, voluntary *Grémios* after 50 per cent of the enterprise in the given sector agreed to join. Once recognized by the Ministry of Corporations, such a *Grémio* was granted a representational monopoly and formal access to various advisory and deliberative councils. These were, however, far from free and autonomous groups. Not only did they have to obey the general rules laid down by the National Labor Code, present their elected officials and annual financial reports for ministerial ratification (or suffer intervention), they were further warned that they 'must subordinate their interests to the interests of the national economy, in collaboration with the State and superior corporative organizations' (Art. 13). In order to prevent any spontaneously formed class alliances, the initiative in founding federations or 'unions' of *Grémios* was left to the state. Voluntary *Grémios*, however, were empowered to elaborate 'special regulations' (read production or marketing cartel arrangements), but these only became legally binding upon approval of the Corporative Council.[24] In short, voluntary employer *Grémios* may have been legally the freest agents in Portuguese corporatism, but they were far from having the autonomy presupposed by the pluralist system of interest representation.

Unfortunately, consistent serial data on the formation of employer *Grémios* are not publicly available. Detailed breakdowns by type, sector and membership only cover the last decade. Nevertheless, episodic information suggests that Portuguese industrial and commercial employers, especially the former did not rush to form voluntary *Grémios.* By the late 1950s very important industrial sectors, e.g. metal-working, cotton textiles and cork, had yet to 'corporatize' themselves. These tended to express their interests from within the specialized 'sectors' of the old Industrial Associations in Lisbon and Porto. The subsequent creation (from above and by decree) of the Corporations after 1956 seems to have belatedly triggered an associational response on their part. By 1967 there were 559 *Grémios* in metropolitan Portugal (as against 324 *Sindicatos* and 695 *Casas do Povo*). Ninety-One of these were obligatory (35 in industry, 43 in commerce, transportation and communications, 13 in agriculture); 467 were voluntary (53 in industry and 191 in commerce). The remainder of the so-called voluntary guilds (226) were *Grémios da Lavoura* or agricultural landowners' guilds. These formed yet another distinct category of the extremely complex legal structure of Portuguese corporatism.

After the major initial decrees discussed above, very few large-scale changes were made until the late 1950s. Instead the regime merely extended the system to cover sectors originally 'overlooked'. In 1937 it announced the establishment (by decree and at its initiative) of *Casas dos Pescadores,* 'Houses for the Fishermen'. Like the Houses of the People, these had a deliberately mixed (employer-worker), involuntary membership and financial support, but unlike its predecessor, the president of the Casa was openly and directly appointed by the State.[25] These formed quickly and for year there were 28 of them, one in each fishing port.

The only economic sector remaining was rural landowners. They had been impressed into the *Casas do Povo* and controlled them. Nevertheless, these were not, strictly speaking, representative-regulative bodies. Some major commodity sectors, e.g., wheat, wine and fruits, had quickly been regimented into obligatory *Grémios*, but this still left large numbers of less specialized producers 'unprotected' and 'unincorporated'. Given the regime's integralist 'horror of the vacuum', it moved in 1937 to fill the gap with yet another set of institutions, the *Grémios da Lavoura.* Once set up by the state or individual initiative in a given *frequesia* or district, membership automatically became mandatory for all. The usual ministerial controls over elections, political activity and financial accounting were imposed, but the regime went even further. Agricultural guilds could only be created by landowners who paid more than a certain minimum amount of taxes and who were not simultaneously salaried. As if this were not enough to ensure that they would not fall into the hands of the very numerous class of medium and small peasants, access to the general council of these *Grémios* was reserved for 'the twenty largest producers residing in a given area' plus some representatives elected by the other producers (Art. 31, Decree No. 29494).[26]

Data on the historical proliferation of *Grémios da Lavoura* are scanty but suggest a pattern similar to that of the *Sindicatos Nacionais*: rapid increase in number from the point of initiation (1937) to approximately 1945, then stagnation. In 1954 there were 231 of them scattered more or less evenly over the metropolitan territory. By 1967 the number had decreased to 226.

THE EVOLUTION OF CORPORATIST REPRESENTATION

Portugal is a Corporative State in intention, not in fact. – Marcello Caetano

The first decade of modern Portuguese corporatism was a period of extraordinary activity and continuous experimentation. It produced some twenty decrees establishing a very complex system of representative institutions and political practices which, while skewed to reflect asymmetries in the existing distribution of power and privilege, was firmly in the control of a relatively autonomous state apparatus. Interwoven with it and superordinate to it came a new and greatly expanded array of governmental bureaucratic institutions: the Sub-secretary of State (later Ministry) for Corporations, the National Institute for Labor and Social Welfare (INTPS), a labor court system, an extensive inspectorate and a vast number of functionally specific, para-state boards, regulatory commissions, councils, etc. This 'Corporative complex', along with such parallel institutions as the single dominant party, the *União Nacional.*[27] a paramilitary organization, the *Legião Portuguesa;* a compulsory youth movement, the *Mocidade Portuguesa;* 'welfare' agencies such as the National Foundation for Joy at Work; and an extensive and efficient set of internal security institutions: the *Guarda Nacional Republicana* for rural order, the *Policia de Segurança Pública* for urban order and the *Policia Internacional e de Defesa do Estado* (PIDE) for political order, provided the structural basis for enduring and stable authoritarian rule. The successive 'emergencies' produced by the Great Depression, the Spanish Civil War and World War II, no doubt, were responsible for some of the system's more specific features, although the corporative impetus anticipated and antedated most of these 'conjunctural' forces.

If the Spanish Civil War and anticipated reaction to World War II had a marked effect accelerating the rate of corporatization and inhibiting resistance to it, the war period itself had a more lasting and almost fatal effect on its structure and practices. Although we lack the necessary detailed monographic studies, it appears that the regime made very extensive and autocratic use of corporatist bodies, including the employer *Grémios*, during World War II. Prices were fixed; quotas were allocated; fines were levied; salaries and wages were compressed in large measure under 'corporatist' auspices – along with an expanding set of state agencies and para-state commissions. All pretence of internal autonomy was removed; elections were suspended and leaders appointed and removed from above. In the name of the wartime exigencies, the *Sindicatos, Casas* and *Grémios* were converted into direct agents of the state, and acted only at its convenience and command. The more subtle and indirect manipulatory provisions of the original corporatist system were simply set aside.

In essence, a mockery was made of the two meta-purposes which Portuguese and other corporatists liked to claim as the basis for their contrived system of interest representation: (1) the creation of a natural, organic harmony based on voluntary mutual consent between capital and labor – otherwise made 'artificially' antagonistic by subversive doctrines and partisan enmities; (2) the devolution of decisional authority to functionally specific, self-governing corporations. Instead, control over class relations became completely monopolized and rigidly controlled from above by the state, which itself enormously expanded the scope of its activities and centralized the means by which policies were adopted. Portuguese corporatism instead of leading to a debureaucratization, deconcentration and 'destatification' of the political system, contributed to the contrary.[28]

As a result of this more-or-less manifest perversion of its ideals, and critical attacks by the victorious allies on such a 'fascist' atavism, corporatism in Portugal after World War II fell into disrepute. Actually, none of the leading figures in the régime, least of all Salazar, openly renounced his faith in it. Nevertheless, books, pamphlets and speeches extolling its virtues decreased in frequency of appearance and/or became markedly more defensive in tone.

Total membership in the National Syndicates and 'Houses' had risen rapidly from 1.5 per cent of the total population in 1935 to 9.7 per cent by 1945.[29] Thereafter it stagnated: 10 per cent in 1950, 10.5 per cent in 1955, 10.6 per cent in 1960. As we have already seen, the rate of formation of new corporatist entities declined almost to nil. There was little evidence that consolidation had taken place at the intermediate (federation or 'union') level and, as yet, there were no Corporations. It seemed possible that the regime was prepared to allow the 'Corporative complex' to wither away to be replaced gradually by free and competitive associability.

Then, came a sudden resurgence of interest in corporatism. Salazar in 1950 announced publicly that rumors of its demise were premature and shortly thereafter a number of important ideological-legal treatises were published, reaffirming the 'modernity' and viability of the corporatist enterprise.

This intellectual ferment culminated in 1956 in two new corporatist decrees, the first ones since the 1930s which substantially modified the system. One announced that at long last the Corporations would be formed (by the state); the other sponsored the creation of an ambitious paper plan for the promulgation of corporatist doctrine and the training of new cadres to man the system.

Unlike a 1938 decree on corporations which 'never left the pages of the *Diário do Governo*' (As Corporações na Economia Nacional, 1971: 37), this time the state moved quickly to establish them. Six 'economic' groups were announced in 1956: (1) Agriculture, (2) Industry, (3) Commerce, (4) Transport and Tourism, (5) Credit and Insurance, (6) Fishing and Canning. Two more were added in 1959: (1) Press and Printing, (2) Entertainment, followed in 1966 by three 'social' Corporations: (1) Welfare, (2) Science, Letters and the Arts, (3) Physical Education and Sports. Formally, all eleven Corporations (actually not all were functioning by 1971) were composed jointly and equally of representatives from worker and employer guilds, syndicates, federations and 'unions', but it appears that all corporation presidents were and had been employers. Interview contacts with supposed representatives of working class syndicates to Governing Councils indicated that these tended to be liberal professionals: lawyers, engineers and managers who under the Portuguese classification system were considered 'workers'. In short, it would have been misleading to describe these new peak associations as instruments of active class collaboration. Much of their rather modest activity was devoted to matters of interest to employers, mostly the elaboration of technical reports and the transmission of governmentally-supplied information. A published summary of their activities since the early 1960s clearly indicated that they had yet to find an active place in the policy-making process, (As Corporações na Economia Nacional, 1971: 173)[30] despite an effort in 1969 by the regime to provide them with some role in arbitrating deadlocked wage and salary negotiations (Lucena, 1971: Vol. 2, *passim*). Formerly, this had been the exclusive province of the Ministry of Corporations.

The placing of these formal capstones to the system, the proliferation of new ideological publications and legal treatises, the establishment of various schools and institutes for the training and indoctrination of new leaders, some evidence of an increase in the number of *Grémios* and rise in the syndicalized proportion of the total population (from 10.5 per cent in 1960 to 11.9 per cent in 1965), plus the reiterated political support of Salazar's successor, Marcello Caetano, seemed to indicate that corporatism was not only alive but flourishing in contemporary Portugal. From the doldrums of the 1940s and 1950s it appeared to have emerged, rejuvenated, as a major structural and ideological component of 'modernized' authoritarian rule.

Appearance, however can be deceptive. It could be argued that the future of Portuguese corporatism had never been more precarious. In the past, its failure to achieve the stated goals of spontaneous class collaboration and functional self-government could always be dismissed on the ground that the system had not yet been completed – the Corporations had not yet been formed – due to circumstances beyond authoritarian control, or so they claimed. Finally, the system's bluff was being called. Virtually, the entire organizational structure was in place and, after forty years, it was becoming more difficult to claim that its shortcomings were due to external disturbances or the absence of trained and properly conscious leaders. The excuses for rigid state tutelage had been exhausted.

And yet there came no sign that decisional authority was being devolved from the Ministries and para-state Boards, Institutes and Agencies to the Corporations, that governmental controls over internal autonomy were going to be removed,[31] that corporatist ideals had become accessible to and accepted by the masses, or, for that matter even by leading propertied elites. In short, while comparatively speaking, Portugal may have been the most corporative state in existence, it had yet to become corporative in terms of values and goals set by its own doctrine. Nowhere is this made more obvious than by examining the role of corporative representation in the policy process.

THE ROLE OF CORPORATISM IN THE POLICY PROCESS

> *Fortunately, in Portugal everything is already institutionalized.* – O. Salazar

By some theories of political development, this boast of Salazar would have made Portugal one of the most developed polities in existence – as well as one of the most persistent and stable. How, then, did corporatist representation fit into such a highly institutionalized order? We have already seen that, ideological claims to the contrary notwithstanding, the Portuguese economy was not 'self-governing' and the polity not 'functionally decentralized'. What, short of accomplishing these 'ideal' goals, had been the influence of corporatism on public policy? Where, how and to what extent did these Syndicates, Guilds, 'Houses', Federations, 'Unions' and Corporations control the direction of political change?

The tentative answer would appear to be: very little. Of course, we totally lack the monographs on specific issue arenas where *clientela*-type arrangements may have prevailed, or even on general policy decisions where the support or resistance of corporatist bodies may have been crucial. But in open, exploratory interviews with association leaders, high government officials and knowledgeable outsiders, the opinion was virtually unanimous that the 'Corporative Complex' was not very influential. Occasionally, it was credited with a certain 'nuisance value', i.e. with being able to prevent decisions from being taken or made effective which the regime was not fully sure it wanted to take anyway (e.g. agrarian reform) or to protect existing privileges from encroachment by modernizing-rationalizing initiatives (e.g. wheat, other commodities, certain 'conditioned' industrial sectors).

Over time the general policy-making process in Portugal gradually shifted. Until the 1960s, it might be described as a heavily personalist, executive-centered coalition or 'court' system in which Salazar surrounded himself with a set of trusted individuals and personal acquaintances, each of whom 'represented' a distinct functional hierarchy: the Church, the armed forces, high finance, industry, the professorate, agriculture, fishing, the government party, the civil bureaucracy (Rudel, 1968: 81-82; Garnier, 1952: *passim*). The power and status of these representatives did not depend on having attained specific positions in the 'Corporative Complex', although some occasionally did hold these offices, just as they moved in and out of ministerial posts. In the latter years of his reign and more rapidly since Marcello Caetano took over in 1968, the role of these ageing 'cronies' had been partially replaced by a relatively efficient and younger group of technocrats attached directly to the President of the Council. Intersectoral and interministerial planning commissions and working groups became the most important sources of policy initiatives, many of which were aimed at liberalizing or removing the heavily regulative, sectorial restrictions implanted during the 1930s and 1940s (de la Sonchére, 1970; Allemann, no date, 7-23; The Economist, 1968; 42-43). Here, the system largely bypassed or ignored the 'Corporative Complex', rather than manipulating or co-opting it as formerly.

In short, neither 'model' of authoritarian decision-making, the personalist or the technocratic, allocated a major policy role to corporatist institutions as such. In the former, this could be 'explained' by the incompleteness of representational structures and the absence of an appropriate 'mentality'. In the latter, as economic bureaucrats and state planning officials deal directly with firms, producers and (rarely) workers or consumers, the positive role of such structures became even more problematic.

Formally speaking, corporatist representation 'plugged into' the decisional system at four levels in accordance with the stated constitutional principle: 'Our Corporative institutions will be organically represented in all activities of the Nation' (Art. 20):

(1) The local *Grémios, Sindicatos* and *Casas* participated in the election of municipal officials. While there was some evidence that this facilitated a certain overlap in authority structures (and provided some degree of status gratification as *Grémio* leaders often became municipal councilmen) at the lowest level in the system, there was virtually *no* evidence that these municipalities exercised decisional autonomy or controlled access to important resources.[32] Hence, whatever clout the corporative system may have acquired here would be of only minor policy significance. Its payoff was most likely realized by individual participants.

(2) The public administration of Portugal was riddled with large numbers of consultative commissions, advisory councils, boards, etc., on which sat permanently designated representatives of corporatist institutions. This, undoubtedly, was the primary decisional arena to which their attention was directed and within which their influence was felt. While we do not, as mentioned above, know much about their role in fixing support prices, setting quotas, allocating subsidies, 'conditioning' the locale, type and extent of industrial investment, etc., we can assume that, whatever their clout in these micro-economic areas, the broad lines of macro-economic policy were set elsewhere. Their influence was, therefore, effectively confined to minor modifications of lines of policy established elsewhere (Schmitter, 1971: 317-365). Interestingly, representational forums formally created to advise the government on such broad lines, e.g. the Consultative Council on Economic Policy, never met.

(3) In 1959 the mode of election of the President of the Republic (formerly, a more or less figurehead position, but formally the head of state and the man who picks the President of the Council of Ministers who is the effective leader of the government) was changed, making it indirect.[33] In the electoral college, members of the Corporative Chamber and municipal officials (many of whom are *Grémio* and *Casa* leaders)

participated. Since this was an act of pure formality, it was difficult to see how corporative leaders could exploit this newly acquired role to sectoral advantage.

To the extent that the official government party played an important role in chief executive selection (a doubtful assumption),[34] the corporative system was again locked out. The *União Nacional* was never internally structured, *a la mexicana,* on corporatist principles and indeed relatively few corporatist leaders were party members. Territorial and functional representation were rather sharply differentiated at the national level, despite the overlap at the municipal level.

(4) Finally, the official interest group system was represented in the Corporative Chamber *(Cámara Corporativa).* This was perhaps the most prominent feature of the Portuguese system. In fact, Portugal was institutionally unique in this respect, although other polities (e.g. Spain, Ireland and Ecuador) allocate a few seats in their national legislature to functional representatives.

The existence of the *Cámara* was an integral part of Portugal's claim to being a distinctive corporative state, but certain features of its policy role and internal composition throw considerable doubt on the significance of this claim. Most importantly, the opinions *(pareceres)* of the Chamber were strictly 'advisory'. They could be (and were occasionally) ignored in subsequent deliberation by the Executive and the Legislative Assembly. Also, since a great deal of 'legislation' was decreed directly by the executive power during the nine months the Assembly was not in session and since few of these decrees ever were referred to it, the Chamber only examined a restricted range of total decisional output. Nevertheless, informants agreed that most of the important policy innovations involving legal changes were referred to the Chamber and that its 'advisory opinions' did have an increasing impact on executive amendments.[35] Although legally incompetent, the Chamber had been politically influential – some felt more so than the Assembly itself.

The reason for this became more apparent when one looked at its composition. The bulk of its membership was appointed directly by the government from elected municipal councilmen and officials of the continental and colonial, civil and military administrations. Until 1960 even the approximately one-third of its members who represented corporatist bodies were selected from above, on the grounds that the *Corporaçoes* were not yet functioning. Since then, this component was elected by the respective Corporations.

In short, the Corporative Chamber was not exclusively a representative body accountable to organized, if officially recognized, interest associations. At best, only a small minority fell into that category and the régime had already exercised strict controls over their initial election – if not appointed them outright. Most of the Chamber's *procuradores* were either administrative officials of the régime or local notables acceptable to it. It more closely resembled a sort of National Honor Society or functional-administrative-intellectual College of Cardinals who had been anointed for their service to the State.

Given this peculiar composition, one could argue that an examination of the Corporative Chamber in Portugal affords a virtually unique opportunity to peer into and analyze the dynamics of elite formation in an authoritarian system of political domination. In a way such an analysis might be more valid and illuminating than similar studies of the more authentically representative composition of democratic assemblies. Here, for Portugal, one can argue that the Chamber represented precisely those interests, collective and individual, which Salazar (and subsequently Caetano) wished to reward for their fidelity to the system, or to coopt in an attempt to ensure their future fidelity. The mechanism of choice lay firmly in their hands.

Table 5 displays some details of background data on *procuradores* (members) of the Corporative Chamber.[36] In parentheses are entered equivalent data, where available, for the members *(deputados)* of the Legislative Assembly.

First, it is important to observe that the total size of the Chamber increased almost monotonically from an original 108 (1934-38) to 215 (1965-69). Hence, despite the relative constancy of certain proportions, the absolute cell frequencies for these categories increased.

Rubric I (Place of Birth) illustrates that the Chamber had a metropolitan bias, a proportion greater than that in the population as a whole and that in the Legislative Assembly. Diachronically, however, this urban-centeredness tended to decrease. Especially striking was the drop in representatives born in Porto.

Occupationally speaking, the Corporative Chamber was hardly a faithful mirror of the functional structure of Portuguese society – but then, few if any national assemblies are. Urban workers (mostly non-manual) formed a steady 10 per cent of the early sessions, but doubled their proportional representation in 1957-1961. Since then their number declined, but it still represented a sizeable group. Unfortunately, the occupational breakdown of deputies in the Assembly was not comparable but it would appear that very few, if any, of them were workers.

Military officers had a declining proportional representation in the

TABLE 5: BACKGROUND OF 'PROCURADORES' OF THE CORPORATIVE CHAMBER: 1934-69

SESSION		1a.	2a.	3a.	4a.	5a.	6a.	7a.	8a.	9a.
	Member Characteristics (% of Total Membership)	1934-38	1938-42	1942-46	1946-49	1949-53	1953-57	1957-61	1961-65	1965-69
I.	PLACE OF BIRTH									
	Lisbon	27.2	23.4	31.6	30.6	29.8	29.4	23.3	23.3	19.1
	Porto	10.9	9.0	8.5	8.2	9.9	6.3	6.0	5.7	5.1
	("Metropolitans")	(24.0)	(30.7)	(23.9)	(26.0)	(23.7)	(23.7)	(22.5)	(18.7)	
II.	OCCUPATION									
	Workers	10.2	11.7	6.9	9.0	9.2	11.9	20.7	15.3	14.9
	Military Officers	9.3	8.1	8.5	7.5	9.2	7.5	6.4	5.7	4.2
		(15.5)	(13.3)	(14.4)	(16.6)	(15.8)	(15.8)	(12.5)	(8.5)	
	Professors	15.7	14.4	17.9	20.1	15.6	14.4	9.1	12.7	14.0
		(7.7	(11.1)	(7.7)	(7.5)	(14.2)	(00.0)	(6.7)	(5.4)	
	Engineers	9.3	10.8	13.7	11.9	8.5	13.1	8.6	8.7	11.2
		(10.0)	(7.7)	(3.3)	(2.5)	(4.2)	(8.3)	(8.3)	(9.2)	
	Physicians	3.7	8.1	5.1	5.2	5.7	6.9	6.0	4.4	0.2
		(5.5)	(8.8)	(7.7)	(10.8)	(9.2)	(9.2)	(11.7)	(11.5)	
	Lawyers, Judges	6.5	6.3	12.0	11.2	6.4	7.5	14.2	14.8	12.6
		(30.0)	(34.5)	(37.7)	(30.0)	(25.0)	(20.8)	(20.0)	(20.8)	
	Other Liberal Profes-sionals	11.1	10.8	12.8	11.9	10.6	12.5	9.5	13.5	15.8
	Landowners	7.4	8.1	9.4	9.0	7.8	5.0	8.2	12.2	8.8
		(11.0)	(9.9)	(9.9)	(10.8)	(4.1)	(6.6)	(9.2)	(6.9)	
	Industrialists	14.8	10.8	6.0	6.7	11.3	12.5	11.2	9.2	9.3
		(0.0)	(0.0)	(0.0)	(0.0)	(0.0)	(0.8)	(0.8)	(1.5)	
	Merchants	8.3	10.8	9.4	8.2	5.7	6.9	7.3	6.6	6.5
		(0.0)	(1.1)	(0.0)	(3.3)	(3.3)	(0.8)	(1.6)	(2.3)	

TABLE 5: *continued*

III.	GOVERNMENT EMPLOYMENT									
	Ex-Ministers	13.0	10.8	12.0	9.0	9.2	10.6	7.8	8.3	8.4
	Subsecretaries, Rectors, Chefes de Gabinete	18.5	12.6	14.5	14.2	9.9	11.3	10.3	14.8	11.6
	Middle Level	13.9	16.2	20.5	20.1	21.3	17.5	8.6	10.0	10.2
IV.	LOCAL ADMINISTRATION									
	Ex-Civil Governor	4.6	4.5	5.1	3.0	5.7	3.1	3.0	3.9	3.3
	Municipal Councilmen, etc.	21.4	26.1	23.9	24.6	19.5	20.6	21.6	25.3	20.9
V.	MEMBERS OF LEGISLATIVE ASSEMBLY									
	in Republic	17.6	11.7	6.8	5.2	5.0	2.5	1.3	0.9	0.5
	in Estado Novo	0.9	2.7	6.0	5.2	7.1	6.9	7.8	7.0	10.2
VI.	COLONIAL EXPERIENCE									
	Public Administration	9.3	9.9	8.5	5.2	5.7	5.6	4.7	8.7	9.3
	Private Business	1.9	0.0	2.6	4.5	5.7	5.0	4.3	2.6	5.1
VII.	MEMBERS OF UNIAO NACIONAL	5.6	8.1	11.1	11.2	15.6	11.3	13.8	13.5	13.5
VIII.	MEMBERS OF PORTUGUESE LEGION, PORTUGUESE YOUTH	1.9	0.9	4.3	6.7	5.7	8.8	11.6	10.9	7.9
	N =	(108)	(111)	(117)	(134)	(141)	(160)	(232)	(229)	(215)

Chamber (although their absolute number was more or less constant). They were much more prominent in the composition of the Assembly. Obversely, professors and engineers were much more "represented" in the Chamber, having held down a large and constant proportion of the seats there.

The traditional liberal professionals, lawyers and physicians with their natural clientéles and high local status prospered more in the electoral-promotional current than in the functional-representative one. For years, lawyers and judges constituted almost one third of the Assembly, but never more than 15 per cent of the Corporative Chamber.

Those who emphasize the regime's accountability to rural or landed interests may be surprised to note that these accounted for only 7 to 10 per cent of either the *procuradores* or *deputados.* Actually, the *curriculum vitae* of many of the physicians and lawyers, as well as some of the industrialists and merchants, suggested strong linkages with the rural sector. Agrarian interests were, therefore, not as under-represented as Table 5 would seem to indicate.

Industrialists and merchants (often hard to distinguish from each other in Portugal) did not form a large 'bourgeois block' in the Chamber, although their proportional representation hovered in the 15 to 20 per cent range. They were, however, almost completely absent from the Legislative Assembly. Clearly, corporatism gave to these sectors a prominence, if not an influence, which they would not have been likely to gain through the electoral process – even one as closed as the Portuguese.

The key to understanding the 'responsible' operation of the Chamber is to be found in the substantial number of ex-ministers, high civil servants, university rectors, and middle-level government employees among its members. If we add to these the Civil Governors of continental and overseas provinces (many of whom were military personnel), we discover (see Table 6) that exactly one half of those present in the first Chamber session have held or were holding such exalted official positions. Their proportion only barely decreased until the Seventh Session (1957-61) when the total number of *procuradores* rose substantially bringing an influx of workers and lawyers. However, even for the most recent session for which data have been processed, one third of those sitting in the Chamber were or had been important direct agents of the State and hence closely attached to the régime itself.

Although the data are perhaps a bit less reliable, the biographies of *procuradores* did indicate a slight overlap of roles with the system of territorial or electoral representation. Ex-deputies (or senators) from the previous republican regime formed a sizeable proportion of the corporative

TABLE 6: PERCENTAGE OF 'PROCURADORES' OF THE CORPORATIVE CHAMBER WHO WERE HIGHER CIVIL SERVANTS: 1934-69

SESSION	1a.	2a.	3a.	4a.	5a.	6a.	7a.	8a.	9a.
1934-38	1934-38	1938-42	1942-46	1946-49	1949-53	1953-57	1957-61	1961-65	1965-69
I. Ministers, Subsecretaries, Chefes de Gabinete, Civil Governors, Middle-level Executives	50.3	44.1	52.1	46.3	46.1	42.5	29.7	37.0	33.5
II. University Professors*	15.7	14.4	17.9	20.1	15.6	14.4	9.1	12.7	14.0
III. Military Officers*	9.3	8.1	8.5	7.5	9.2	7.5	6.4	5.7	4.2

*Since a substantial number of the University professors and military officers have also been ministers, subsecretaries, etc., the percentages for the categories are not additive.

representatives in the first sessions – although death and old age dwindled their numbers. They were, in a sense, replaced by a steadily growing percentage of representatives who had been *deputados* in the Assembly of the Estado Novo. This is also reflected in the number of *procuradores* who reported holding positions in the National Union, the Portuguese Legion and/or the Portuguese Youth. This might be interpreted either as evidence for the emergence of a pattern of elite crystallization and internal reinforcement, or as evidence for elite circulation as newcomers found these party and para-military channels useful for worming their way into the annointed circle.

Finally, the breakdowns suggest that the Chamber was not a major sounding board for the articulation of colonial interests. A sizeable, but steady, proportion of its members were in administrative positions in the 'overseas provinces'. This seemed to be decreasing until the eighth session (1961-65), which began just at the outbreak of hostilities in Angola, markedly increased their representation. As for the representation of private interests from these provinces, the data forceably grossly underestimate their importance, as I only coded those whose business connections were manifestly tied to firms operating in Angola, Mozambique, etc.

If one accepts the notion that the Corporation Chamber could have been regarded as a sort of National Honor Society in which the regime rewarded those to whom it was beholden or wished to be beholden, then the data suggest that its social centre of gravity was not all that different from that of the parliamentary regime which preceded it, namely the urban petite bourgeoisie. Industrialists and merchants were directly and well represented; rural landowners less so. Manual workers, especially agricultural ones, were almost completely absent; non-manual workers, especially at the supervisory and middle-management level, were respectably present. The most peculiar feature of its occupational representation-cum-support was the extraordinarily sizeable presence of the nation's professors (the *catedratocracia*) and bureaucrats. Admittedly it would be precarious to infer from this alone the *relative* independence of the state apparatus *(der verselbständigte Macht der Executivgewalt)* which Marx stressed so much in his Bonapartist model, but other evidence also points in that direction.[37]

If, however, one considers the Corporative Chamber not as a convenient sample of the annointed elite, but as a policy-making or influencing body, then the message is different. The Chamber was not a major channel through which the "Corporative Complex" made its influence felt. Occasionally, spokesmen for the regime hinted that in the future it would acquire decisional, not just advisory competence and that it would replace the Ministry of Corporations as the general supervisor of the whole corporative system. There was no sign that such outcomes were imminent or even seriously contemplated. As it stood, the Chamber could have been abolished completely and it would neither have radically disturbed the pattern of policy-making, nor seriously threatened the persistence of the 'Corporative Complex'.

CORPORATIST REPRESENTATION AND PUBLIC POLICY IMPACT

> *Without struggle, without harm, without damage, Portuguese workers continued obtaining all the just benefits that in other countries cost the working class and the national economy sacrifices beyond measure.* – Marcello Caetano

While proponents of the Corporative state argued that it saved the country from chaos and benevolently granted from above the welfare and security for which the other working classes of Europe had to struggle, its opponents retorted that authoritarian rule retarded and distorted economic and social development, widening rather than narrowing the gap between Portugal and the rest of Europe. No one (to my knowledge) dared suggest that the implantation of corporatist-authoritarian rule in Portugal made no difference with regard to such policy-related outcomes.

However, amid the recent revival of scholarly interest in the policy consequences of political structural characteristics, one theme has emerged with monotonous regularity: differences between or within regimes are alleged to make little or no difference. The conclusions have tended to be similar whether arrived at by statistical inference from synchronic partial correlations across units, or on descriptive evaluation based on diachronic counter-factual assumptions within units. We have been led to believe that the relatively constant features of ecological setting and underlying class interests and/or the persistence of subtle machinations by informal cliques and patron-client dyads impose such narrow and fixed parameters upon performance that it makes no 'real' difference if political structures are more or less centralized, more or less competitive, or more or less participatory. Such an over-determined system (provided the three layers of determinism are self-reinforcing) will produce the same outputs and outcomes – i.e. benefit the same interests – in any case short of violent revolution.

It is admitted that some professional politicians may lose their jobs, some intellectuals may find it difficult to express their opinions and some subordinate class leaders may spend time in jail or exile, but these are regarded as minor incidents, questions of style or taste, and do not affect the substance of policy itself. The bulk of the subject population will continue to deal in the same way with the same officials and to receive the same policy benefits.

In addition to certain obvious problems involving the selection of variables, operational indicators and analytical techniques (Schmitter, 1972b; Jacob and Lipsky, 1971: 14-40), these conclusions about regime irrelevance are based on a fundamental misspecification of the counterfactual alternative. This is particularly misleading when comparing the policy consequences of authoritarian and liberal-democratic régimes. What is so easily and conveniently ignored is that authoritarian seizures of power from ailing parliamentary democracies were and are usually designed to *prevent* changes from occurring which seemed highly likely or imminent. That they are subsequently successful in restoring 'order' and in placing the country back on its 'proper' position on some long-term trendline – hence, apparently identical to past performance – misses the point. Their policy impact must be assessed relative to the opportunities (or catastrophes) foregone, the changes in output and outcome which might have occurred had the political processes of electoral competition, class representation and state transformation been permitted to run their 'free' course.

This recasting of the framework for evaluating system performance demands either the construction of imaginative (and hence controversial) counterfactual scenarios of what might have happened, within the same country, if the oligarchic, corrupt, indecisive and unstable parliamentary régime had not been replaced by an authoritarian one, or the utilization of carefully selected 'matched comparisons' with other countries sharing certain initial parametric similarities but which maintain open, competitive political structures. I have opted for the latter of these two strategies for inference.

While both the proponents and the opponents of the *Estado Novo* implicitly agree that its performance must be judged in terms of *what did not happen to Portugal,* they differ diametrically as to *what would most likely have happened.* It is difficult enough to find another national polity which was ecologically similar in the mid-1920s but even more difficult to find one which also faced the same sort of political strains as Portugal and, hence, which would potentially satisfy both (divergent) counterfactual scenarios; the conservative one which stresses inexorable economic and

TABLE 7:
PARAMETRIC SIMILARITIES BETWEEN PORTUGAL, SPAIN, IRELAND, FINLAND AND GREECE IN 1930

		Portugal	Spain	Ireland	Finland	Greece
I.	TOTAL POPULATION (in 000.000s)	6.8	23.4	2.9	3.5	6.4
II.	LABOR FORCE					
	Primary Sectors (as % of economically active population)	56.5	45.4	53.5	57.0	51.8
	Secondary Sector (as % of economically active population)	20.5	32.3	13.3	22.6	22.3
	Tertiary Sector (as % of economically active population)	23.0	22.3	33.2	20.4	26.9
III.	URBANIZATION (% of total population in cities over 50,000)	12.1	19.2	15.5	11.7	12.6
IV.	LITERACY (% of total population)	39.5	38.4	90.0 (est)	84.1	57.6
V.	SCHOOL ENROLLMENT (per 100,000)	579	1580	18414	1209	1221
VI.	ELECTRIC POWER PRODUCTION (KWH per capita)	382	1112	334	3496	–
VII.	NATIONAL INCOME (in I.U.)					
	Total (in 000.000s)	860	7510	913	641	1072
	Per capita	127	325	326	210	189
VIII.	FOREIGN TRADE (US $ Imports and Exports per capita)	$37.47	$66.22	$286.84	$131.42	$56.31
IX.	GOVERNMENTAL EXPENDITURES (US $ per capita)	$13.16	$26.63	$49.97	$27.33	$20.10
X.	POLITICAL INSTABILITY (Number of Major Cabinet Changes and changes in Effective Executive: 1920-25)	8	17	7 1922-27	17	27

Sources:
I. Dewhurst, *et al.* (1961).
II. Dewhurst *et al.* (1961): Kennedy (1971); Clark, (1957: 515).
III. Banks (1971).
IV. UNESCO (1967). For Portugal, literacy is defined as the ability to read.
V. Banks (1971).
VI. Banks (1972).
VII. Clark (1957: 88-200).
VIII. Banks (1972).
IX. Banks (1972).

social chaos ensuing from the instability of the late Republic;[38] and the radical one which stresses the self-redeeming and self-transforming qualities of a continuous democratic process.

Four countries emerge from the mid and late 1920s as likely candidates: Spain, Ireland, Finland and Greece. In Table 7 are displayed some data on basic economic, social and political parameters around 1930 for Portugal and these four potential counterfactual 'partners'.

Spain can be quickly excluded on grounds of greater size of population and national income, as well as greater urbanization and a more developed occupational structure, e.g., 32 per cent of the economically active population in industry as opposed to 20.5 per cent in Portugal. When to these are added the effects of protracted civil war and postwar international ostracism, they outweigh the advantages of the obvious cultural and historical similarities between the two units.

Finland provides some striking parallels to Portugal in 1930, not only in occupational structure and urbanization but also in its even higher rate of political instability. Its much higher literacy, school population and electricity production, however, coupled with such factors as international warfare, strategic position, and differing cultural and religious beliefs make it an unlikely match. It does serve, however, as a reminder that high strike rates, electoral, cabinet and executive instability, fiscal deficits and, even extensive paramilitary activity did not always give way to authoritarian rule or fascism. Here, parliamentary rule was capable of riding out the Great Depression and World War II and laying the basis for a modern egalitarian and openly competitive welfare state.

Ireland offers a particularly tantalizing comparison: a heavily Roman Catholic and authoritarian culture (Chubb, 1970: 55-56), an Atlantic maritime geographic setting, a conservative régime with a 'predominant party system" (Chubb, 1970: 73), a heavy dependence on the United Kingdom and massive emigration – all this in addition to an economic and social structural setting around 1930 quite similar to Portugal. The match is not, however, perfect. Ireland was smaller in population, slightly more urbanized and a great deal more literate and schooled. It had a clear initial advantage in per capita income ($326 to $127) and disadvantage, if one is to accept uncritically the fulminations of theorists of international dependence, in its vulnerability to foreign trade ($287 per capita in foreign trade as opposed to $37). Government expenditures per capita in 1930 were easily the highest of the five countries ($30 as opposed to $13 in Portugal). Most importantly, Ireland had not suffered from marked parliamentary or electoral instability since its 1922 independence – although the very incomplete Banks' time-series data record seven major changes of cabinet and effective executive from 1922 to 1927 and only record eight for Portugal from 1920 to 1925.[39] In short, by offering Ireland as a counterfactual standard of comparison for policy performance, one risks biasing one's evaluation in favor of the democratic opponents of the *Estado Novo.*

Greece offers a potential bias in the opposite direction. More politically unstable than Portugal during the 1920s, it too collapsed into authoritarian rule in the late 1930s and, of course, most recently in 1967. Nevertheless, between these episodes and wartime occupation, it managed to sustain a more or less open political process with a sizeable electorate and an accountable executive, although its interest group system remained strikingly similar to that of Portugal: corporatists and authoritarian (Legg, 1969). With virtually no initial advantages over Portugal (except a higher rate of literacy and schooling), Greece before 1967 might well be considered to personify the outcome most feared and studiously avoided by the *Estado Novo:* an unstable parliamentary régime, exposed to subversive ideologies and movements, racked by internal factionalism and endemic violence, exploited by great powers and foreign capitalists, weakened by budgetary unbalance and monetary inflation. If this system did, nevertheless, out-perform Portugal over the long haul, it would be difficult to argue convincingly on other than spiritual or meta-empirical grounds that protracted authoritarian rule was worth it.

In effect, I suppose that we can best evaluate the policy consequences of authoritarian rule in Portugal by means of a quasi-experimental, time series design which includes Ireland and Portugal as contrasting cases.[40] Portugal began its protracted 'experimental treatment in 1928 (actually 1932-34 would be a better starting point for consolidated experimentation). Ireland presents the pure contrast with no such treatment; Greece affords an example of sporadic and interrupted treatment:

TABLE 8: A QUASI-EXPERIMENTAL DESIGN FOR COMPARING POLICY PERFORMANCES IN PORTUGAL, IRELAND AND GREECE

	1920s	1930s	1940s	1950s	1960s	1970s
			Neutrality			
Portugal	OOOXX	XXXXX	XXXXX	XXXXX	XXXXX	XXXXX
			Neutrality			
Ireland	OOOOO	OOOOO	OOOOO	OOOOO	OOOOO	OOOOO
			Occupation			
Greece	OOOOO	OOXXX	XXXOO	OOOOO	OOOOO	OOXXX
			Civil War			

FIGURE 1:
HYPOTHETICAL POLICY PERFORMANCE PATHS:
Portugal, Ireland and Greece, 1920-75

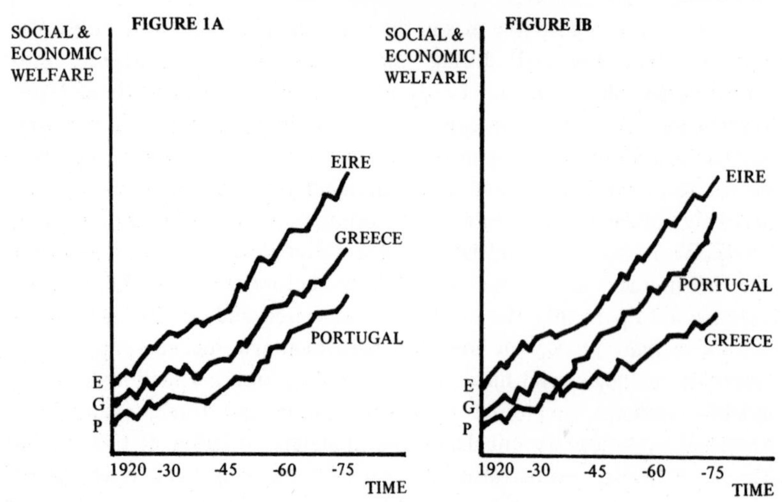

If consistent and reliable data were available on a single valid indicator of social and economic welfare, one could simply plot it over time for all three units and infer from the shifts in trendlines the impact of 'experimental' regime treatments (or their absence in the case of non-treatments). Figure 1 shows several hypothetical plots. In Figure 1a, regime type appears to have had no differentiating impact on welfare. All three countries held their respective positions. Reduction in the slope of the trendline was universally associated with depression and war; short-run upturns and downturns were not coincident with regime change. About all that could be inferred in favor of authoritarian rule from this plot is that the Portuguese indicator performs somewhat less erratically after 1933.

Figure 1b presents the strongest possible (hypothetical) case for a positive evaluation of the *Estado Novo.* Not only did its initiation take the irregularities out of previous performance, but its policies of budgetary balance, fiscal stringency, economic autarky and suppression of political expression permitted Portugal to outperform its 'competitors' during both depression and wartime. Subsequently, in the postwar period, it gained on consistently democratic Ireland, while 'chaotically' democratic Greece languished – at least until it too instituted authoritarian rule.

Figure 1c makes the strongest case against authoritarian rule. Portugal's depression and wartime performance is no better than that of unstable authoritarian (and later occupied) Greece and worse than that of Ireland. Once the war had ended, Greece quickly and definitively overtook Portugal, Ireland forged even farther ahead. Democratic rule, consistent or not is shown (in this hypothetical distribution of the data) clearly more capable of generating higher levels of economic and social welfare.[41]

Of course, inferences from all three pseudo-plots were based on the assumption that nothing happened simultaneously with the implantation of authoritarian rule and that nothing intervened differentially and subsequently in the global environment of one unit that might have produced the same effect. It also presumes that the three units are politically equivalent, in the limited sense that they enjoy some similar range of capability for deciding autonomously how collective resources will be amassed and allocated. None are manifestly satellites or subunits of another polity, although all are dependent to a degree on wider systems of international influence which, no doubt, set limits on 'acceptable' policy alternatives and the impact these are 'permitted' to have.

Needless to say, the data needed to complete the entire proposed quasi-experimental design are not presently or, at least, not conveniently available.[42] Nor for that matter has that single valid indicator for general economic and social welfare yet been devised. Therefore one must plough through a multitude of partial indicators and confine one's observation to a shorter time span. The 1930s can be dismissed not only for lack of data but as a period during which the three units were severely and differentially affected by exogeneous conditions, i.e. international depression. The same can be said of the 1940s when neutrality on the part of Portugal and Ireland, occupation and civil war in Greece certainly had a different impact upon patterns of policy output and outcome. This leaves the 1950s and 1960s which, conveniently, is when the quality and comparability of the data improves markedly. In leaping over some twenty years of performance, however, one obviously tends to increase the number of variables other than regime-type which might have intervened to produce divergent outputs and outcomes. It also overlooks the probability that the generic nature of political domination determined how the system responded to both depression and war, which in turn had a major influence on policy options taken (or missed) in the 1950s and 1960s.

Before looking at those taken, one must first establish that there were, indeed, important regime-related structural differences between the three polities. Table 9 makes this quite clear. Both Portugal and Ireland had a stable electorate; the former's was proportionately quite small, the latter's, rather large. Greece, meanwhile, underwent extraordinary electoral mobilization, from 22.4 to 53.0 per cent of the total population in thirteen years. In electoral non-competitiveness, Portugal was in a class by itself.

As far as unionization/syndicalization is concerned, the differences were less remarkable.[43] Greece's was even smaller than Portugal's although much more combatative, as measured by working days lost in industrial disputes.[44] Nevertheless, as mentioned above, Greece combined (until 1967) a representative system which was relatively open and competitive in partisan terms, but paternalistic and authoritarian with regard to workers' organizations (Jecchinis, 1967; Legg, 1969). What set Portugal apart from Greece was the consistency of its corporatism and its 'integral' coverage of all interest sectors, including employer associations.

Consistently greater centralization of governmental resources was another thing which distinguishes Portugal. Also, unlike the other two, its centralization showed no sign of decreasing.

In overall levels of political activity (as imperfectly measured by the Bank's serial data, 1946-66), Ireland was fairly clearly the most peaceful of the three, except in terms of cabinet and executive changes. Greece, on the other hand, seems to have deserved its reputation as a politically chaotic place. Attempted revolutions, government crises and cabinet shuffles in

TABLE 9: POLITICAL STRUCTURE IN PORTUGAL, IRELAND AND GREECE: 1950-70

		Portugal			Ireland			Greece		
I	**Electoral Mobilization**									
	Total Voting Population in 000s	949	1,001	1,114	1,344	1,238	1,264	1,717	3,863	4,627
	Total Eligible Voting Population in 000s	1,100	1,350	1,810	1,785	1,738	1,683	2,224	5,119	5,663
	Voting Population/Total Population	11.4%	11.0%	11.9%	45.1%	41.8%	43.9%	22.4%	41.2%	53.0%
	Voting Population/Eligible Voters	86.3%	74.1%	61.6%	75.3%	71.3%	75.1%	76.9%	76.2%	81.7%
II.	**Electoral Competitiveness**									
	% of Total Vote to Winning Party	99.3 (1949)	76.4 (1958)	88.0 (1969)	46.3 (1951)	48.3 (1957)	47.8 (1965)	36.5 (1951)	41.2 (1958)	52.7 (1964)
III.	**Unionization**									
	Total Membership in Unions/Syndicates	558 (1950)	656 (1960)	842 (1969)	407 (1955)	507 (1959)	452 (1963)	455 (1955)	485 (1959)	564 (1963)
	Total Union Membership/Total Population	6.5%	7.2%	8.9%	13.9%	17.7%	15.9%	5.7%	5.9%	6.6%
	Working Days Lost in Industrial Disputes in 000s	Strikes illegal – not reported				126 (1958)	784 (1966)		109 (1958)	712 (1966)
IV.	**Centralization**									
	Central Government Share in General Government Revenue	79.4 (1950)	75.9 (1960)	78.9 (1968)	66.8 (1950)	66.2 (1960)	64.6 (1968)	77.8 (1950)	61.4 (1960)	56.1 (1968)
V.	**Government Employment**									
	Total in 000s									
VI.	**Political Activity**									
	Assasinations, Riots	9			0			22		
	General Strikes, Anti-Government Demonstrations	3			3			8		
	Attempted Revolutions, Successful Coups, Guerilla Warfare	7			2			10		
	Government Crises, Purges	10			3			24		
	Major Cabinet Changes, Changes in Affective Executive	10			14			41		

Sources:
I, II. Banks, (1972); *Keesing's Contemporary Archives* (appropriate years); PEP, European Political Parties, (1970: 463); Maynaud (1965: 93-125).
III. Portugal, *Anvario Estatistico* (various editions), ILO, *Yearbook* (appropriate years).
IV. IBRD, *World Tables,* Jan 1971.
V. Banks (1972).

Portugal have not been as infrequent as many might have supposed, but they have all been relatively minor affairs and have not attracted much outside notice.

These differences in structure and activity were paralleled by major differences in policy outputs. If central government expenditures as a percent of GNP can be taken as a crude indicator of the role of the state, Ireland and Greece began similarly in the 1950s, far ahead of Portugal, and

TABLE 10: PUBLIC POLICY OUTPUTS IN PORTUGAL, IRELAND AND GREECE: 1950-70

	Portugal			Ireland			Greece		
	1950	**1960**	**1967-69**	**1950**	**1960**	**1967-69**	**1950**	**1960**	**1967-69**
I. Total General Government Expenditures									
A. As % of GNP	10.9	11.3	13.2	21.0	21.4	25.0	21.3	20.0	29.2
B. In US $ per capita	20.51	40.49	63.20 (1966)	92.44	159.64	307.91	61.58	73.82	140.46 (1966)
II. Public Investment									
A. As % of GNP Gross Domestic Investment	11.2	17.4	18.7	16.2	15.1	20.5	16.7	22.9	24.3
B. 1. Private Sector	81.2	79.4		74.8	78.7		74.0	71.9	
2. Public Sector	18.8	20.6		25.2	21.3		26.0	28.1	
TOTAL	100.0 (1951-60)	100.0 (1961-67)		100.0 (1951-60)	100.0 (1961-67)		100.0 (1951-60)	100.0 (1961-67)	
C. Public Savings as % of Public Investment	134.0 (1951-60)	68.2 (1961-67)					4.4 (1951-60)	43.3 (1961-67)	
III. Resource Extraction									
A. Direct Taxes									
1. Households	8.2	9.1	8.5	12.8	13.5	17.4	14.3	13.0	10.5
2. Social Security Contrib.	18.8	19.7	18.3	4.5	4.4	7.5	16.3	22.1	22.5
3. Corporations	21.2	19.7	17.6	8.1	5.8	6.7		1.9	1.6
B. Indirect Taxes	44.7	44.7	47.8	65.8	66.8	60.9	65.3	55.3	58.5
C. Non-Tax Revenue	7.1	6.8	7.8	8.8	9.5	7.5	4.1	7.7.	6.9
TOTAL	100.0	100.0	100.0	100.0	100.0	100.0	100.0	100.0	100.0
D. Total General Government Revenue as % of GNP	18.1 (1953-60)	20.0 (1961-7)	21.3 (1968)	25.0 (1953-60)	27.4 (1961-7)	31.6 (1968)	17.2 (1953-60)	20.2 (1961-7)	24.8 (1968)
IV Sectoral Expenditures									
A. As % of Total General Government Current Expenditure									
1. Civil	43.2	44.4	32.2	44.7	44.2	41.3	30.6	38.1	32.6
2. Defense	26.9	26.9	41.1	8.0	5.5	4.0	29.0	25.5	20.6
3. Subsidies	9.0	5.6	6.1	12.7	13.4	16.1	11.3	2.2	5.6
4. Transfers	16.4	19.4	17.2	25.9	25.2	26.0	29.1	32.6	37.9
5. Payment on Public Debt.	4.5 (1953)	3.7	3.4 (1968)	8.7	11.7	12.6 (1968)		1.6	3.3
B. As % of GNP									
1. Defense	3.8	6.8	7.5	1.5	1.3	1.2	5.3	4.0	5.1
2. Education	1.3 (1953-60)	1.6 (1961-7)	1.6 (1968)	3.1 (1953-60)	3.9 (1961-7)	5.1 (1968)	1.4 (1953-60)	1.9 (1961-7)	2.5 (1968)

Sources:
IBRD, *World Tables* (Jan 1971) except for I.B. which is from Banks *et al.* (1971).

increased their margin during the 1960s. The disparity was even more noticeable when translated into US dollars since, as we shall see, Portugal's GNP was smaller as is its proportional government expenditure. Ireland began with a $72 edge and increased it to over $240; Greece's marginal advantage went from $41 to $76 by 1967-69. The relative weakness of the *Estado Novo* was also reflected in the investment arena. Over-all investment was lower (but improving on Ireland, if not on Greece) and the public sector provided only 19 to 21 per cent of the total. One reason for this is shown in the data on public saving as a percent of public investment. While Portugal in the 1950s saved more than it invested, Greece invested vastly more than it was currently saving. This conservative, pre-Keynesian practice on the part of Salazar was relaxed a bit in the 1960s, but it still served to restrict the active role of the Portuguese state in promoting development.

A breakdown of how these public and private investments were distributed (about 1955) shows a rather striking proportional similarity, reflecting perhaps the general similarity in economic level and structure. Portugal and Ireland were again shown to be the least state capitalist; Portugal the least capable of extracting resources. It, however, was putting more of its gross non-residential investment into manufacturing, mining and construction, along with public administration. Greece was

TABLE 11: PATTERNS OF CAPITAL INVESTMENT IN PORTUGAL, IRELAND AND GREECE, 1955

	Portugal	Portugal	Ireland	Greece
I.	As % of GNP			
	Residential	3.0	2.3	4.9
	Non-Residential	11.1	11.4	9.1
	Changes in Stock	0.4	1.9	1.2
	Net Foreign Balance	-4.3	-8.6	-5.2
	Total Investment	14.5	15.6	15.2
II.	In US$ per capita	$30	$80	$39
III.	% Public	13	15	28
	% Private	87	85	72
IV.	% Gross Non-Residential Investment in			
	Agriculture	14	13	14
	Manufacturing, Mining, Construction	27	17	19
	Public Utilities	16	19	9
	Transport and Communications	22	22	32
	Public Administration	8	5	3
	Other Services	13	24	23

Source: J. F. Dewhurst, *et al.* (1961: 443-78).

concentrating on transport (shipping?), and 'other services'; Ireland on public utilities and 'other services'. In short, despite its less impressive public output performance, Portugal seemed to be employing a strategy aimed at catching up in longer-run developmental outcome.

The pattern of governmental resource extraction provides a hint as to who is paying the bill. Particularly striking is the substantial role that social security contributions from workers play in the fiscal picture of Portugal and Greece. Almost one fifth of the total resources of both regimes was extracted from this source and less than 10 per cent in Ireland. But if we consider that direct taxes on corporations represent an 'equivalent sacrifice' on the part of the bourgeoisie, we find that an extremely small proportion of total revenue came from this source in Greece (0.0 per cent in 1950, 1.9 per cent in 1960, 1.6 per cent in 1968), while in Ireland at least until 1968 their taxes surpassed social security contributions. In Portugal, however, corporations appeared to be relatively heavily taxed, although this burden tended to decline in relative importance (21.2 per cent in 1950, 19.7 per cent in 1960, 17.6 per cent in 1968). Also, indirect taxes with their regressive incidence were proportionately lowest in Portugal. The income of households was most important as a source of governmental revenue in Ireland, least important in Portugal.

Overall, the comparison of resource extraction patterns leads to the fairly conclusive inference that its class incidence was most unequal in Greece, least unequal in Portugal, with Ireland somewhere in between. While this forces one to ponder about the likely class basis of support for the respective regimes, before making any such assumptions, one should examine the distribution and presumed beneficiaries of these funds by sector in order to determine (crudely) the overall incidence of public policy effects.

Section IV of Table 10 clearly illustrates the core of the sectoral distribution problem in Portugal: the enormous importance of military expenditures. Forty-three per cent of the 1968 governmental expenditures, 7.5 per cent of that year's GNP was spent on defense. Ireland only spent 9.1 per cent and 1.2 per cent respectively. Greece, however, demonstrates that maintenance of an overseas empire was not the only motive for high military expenditures. In fact prior to 1960, i.e. prior to the outbreak of guerrilla warfare in Angola, Mozambique and Guinea, Greece was spending proportionately about as much as Portugal in this category. Nevertheless, the Salazar regime even previous to 1961 had been allocating a major proportion of its resources for external security purposes – despite an international and internal context by no means as overtly threatening to regime persistence as that of Greece. This was one of the clear and persistent costs of authoritarian rule and one of such magnitude that it reduced the capacity of public institutions to operate in other policy arenas – if they had wanted to.

Unfortunately, we lack available data on these other arenas, except for education, where Portugal's poor public effort was manifest. Ireland inherited a rather developed educational system for its level of economic development from the British, but has subsequently amplified its levels of support for this public good. Greece and Portugal were and still are far behind. Both increased their educational efforts during the sixties, Greece more so than Portugal.

TABLE 12
SOCIAL SECURITY PROGRAMS AND EXPENDITURES IN PORTUGAL, IRELAND AND GREECE, ca. 1954

	Portugal	Ireland	Greece
Expenditures (in US$ per capita)			
1. Medical Care and Sickness Cash Benefits	$2.80	$14.30	$3.20
2. Old Age Pensions	2.70	16.40	4.20
3. Family Allowances	1.80	5.05	0.00
4. Unemployment Benefits	0.00	3.95	0.45
5. Public Assistance	0.73	0.53	0.18
6. Administrative Costs	1.27	2.47	0.92
TOTAL	9.30	42.70	8.95
As % of GNP	4.6%	8.7%	4.0%

Source: Dewhurst, (1961: 375-403).

In the absence of similar data for general social security spending, I have included a detailed breakdown (about 1955) according to per capita $ benefits expended by functional category. While Portugal and Greece, as we noted, derived about one fifth of their total governmental revenue from social security contributions, Table 12 shows that they distributed much less. Portugal pulled slightly ahead by virtue of its fairly extensive family allowance program, which Greece did not have. The latter, on the other hand, did offer unemployment insurance. Portugal spent more on public assistance, but its 35 cent per capita edge over Greece was exactly accounted for by higher administrative costs. It would appear, however, that in both cases social security programs were a device to transfer resources *away* from the working class.

TABLE 13: HOUSING PROGRAMS IN PORTUGAL, IRELAND AND GREECE, ca. 1955

	Portugal	Ireland	Greece
1. Average Annual Dwelling Units Completed per 100 inhab.	3.1	3.6	6.5
2. Investment in Residential Construction			
% of GNP	3.2	2.7	4.8
US$ per capita	6.90	14.00	14.00
3. Dwellings Receiving Public Aid as % of All New Dwellings Completed	2	97	27
4. % New Dwellings Receiving Public Funds	3	75	5
5. % of New Dwellings Built by Public Agencies	5	54	26

Source: Dewhurst, *et al.* (1961: 213-275).

Finally, we can take a single look (about 1955) at a policy arena which Portuguese authorities emphasized in their propaganda: public housing. Despite Salazar's emphasis on providing individual dwellings for the lower classes and some substantial programs in the 1930s, by 1955 the role of public authorities there was far below that of Ireland and Greece.

As we now turn to policy *outcomes*, 'the consequences traceable to outputs, however long the discernable chain of causation' (Easton, 1965: 349-352), we cannot, however, completely absolve the political system from all responsibility. Obviously, the general performance of the economy and society responds not only to how the public sector spends or does not spend, but also upon the myriad of legal regulations, non-monetary incentives and moral images established by authorities. This is not to say that all outcomes can be linked to definite policy outputs which can in turn be attributed to differences in regime-type. Obviously, a great deal depends on the prevailing cultural, social and economic contexts, although to a degree we have attempted to control for them through our matched comparisons.

Given the quantity of information in Table 14 let me simply summarize its contents briefly and concentrate on the highlights. On most of the measures of per capita social or economic performance Portugal begins the series with a large comparative disadvantage over Ireland and a lesser one

TABLE 14: PUBLIC POLICY OUTCOMES IN PORTUGAL, IRELAND AND GREECE: 1950-70

	Portugal			Ireland			Greece		
	1950	**1960**	**19--**	**1950**	**1960**	**19--**	**1950**	**1960**	**19--**
1. **Gross National Product**									
Total, in US$ billions, constant 1964 prices	1.6	2.4	3.8 (1968)	1.7	1.9	2.6 (1968)	2.0	3.5	5.8 (1968)
In constant 1964 US$ per capita	194	279	405 (1968)	578	687	900 (1968)	268	417	663 (1968)
2. **Economic Growth**									
Rate of per capita increase in GDP	3.7 (1951-60)	5.0 (1961-67)	4.2 (1969)	2.2 (1951-60)	3.3 (1961-67)	4.0 (1969)	4.7 (1951-60)	6.7 (1961-67)	7.2 (1969)
3. **Energy Consumption**									
In Kgs. per capita	260	360	532 (1966)	1230	2014	2453 (1966)	220	569	831 (1966)
4. **Urbanization**									
% of Total Population Living in Cities over 50,000	12.6	12.1	12.0 (1966)	22.8	29.1	29.1 (1966)	16.0	28.6	36.5 (1966)
5. **Literacy**									
% of Total Population which can read and write	55.9	61.9	64.2 (1966)	98.5	98.8	99.3 (1966)	73.5	79.7	86.9 (1966)

Table 14 continued

	Portugal			Ireland			Greece		
	1950	1960	19--	1950	1960	19--	1950	1960	19--
6. **School Enrollment**									
Primary School, per 100 Population	7.5	9.6	9.6	15.8	17.7	16.6	11.9	11.1	11.3
Secondary School, per 100 Population	0.6	1.1	2.0	1.6	2.7	3.7	2.7	3.3	4.5
University, per 100 Population	.17	.21	.41 (1966)	.27	.38	.52 (1966)	.13	.32	.70 (1966)
7. **Media Exposure**									
Newspaper Circulation per 100 Population	6.7	7.8	6.5	19.3	23.2	24.3	8.3	13.3	17.9
Radios per 100 Population	3.0	9.3	13.2	10.3	17.4	28.3	2.3	8.3	10.9
Television sets per 100 Population			.29 (1969)			1.1 (1969)			.09 (1969)
8. **Caloric Intake**									
Per capita per day	2270	2530	2930 (1968)	3430	3480	3460 (1968)	2500	2940	2900 (1968)
9. **Foreign Trade Dependence**									
Imports as % of GNP	22.0	27.5	27.4	39.4	39.3	42.7	18.6	20.3	21.8
Exports as % of GNP	16.9	22.0	23.9	30.7	33.0	36.2	9.1	10.1	10.2
	(1951-60)	(1961-7)	(1968)	(1951-60)	(1961-7)	(1968)	(1951-60)	(1961-7)	(1968)

Table 14 continued

	Portugal			Ireland			Greece		
	1950	1960	19--	1950	1960	19--	1950	1960	19--
10. Foreign Capital Dependence									
External Public Dept as % of GNP	10.6	10.6 (1961-7)	12.0 (1968)	6.7	7.0 (1961-7)	6.7 (1968)		8.6 (1961-7)	8.4 (1968)
Long-Term Borrowing & Net Foreign Investment									
Private (in $ mil)	2.3	4.0	188.0	–	2.0	46.0	26.7	36.3	203.2
Public (in $ mil)	9.7	–	51.0 (1968)	58.2	9.0	– (1968)	–	24.9	44.3 (1968)
11. International Reserves									
As % of Imports	156.0 (1951-60)	85.3 (1961-7)		11.9 (1951-60)	46.3 (1961-7)		35.1 (1951-60)	29.1 (1961-7)	
12. International Aid									
US Economic and Military Aid (in US$ 000s)		534 (1946-70)			192 (1946-70)			3886 (1946-70)	
IBRD Loans (in US$ 000s)		57.5 (1948-70)			14.5 (1948-70)			46.3 (1948-70)	

Table 14 continued

	Portugal			Ireland			Greece		
	1950	1960	19--	1950	1960	19--	1950	1960	19--
13. Income Distribution									
Wages and Salaries as % of Gross National Income	39.4 (1953-4)	41.0 (1958-9)	44.3 (1963-4)	55.2	55.2	61.0 (1968)		35.4	40.2 (1968)
Land Tenure									
Farms 1-10 ha. as % of Total Farms		89.9 (1950s)			42.8 (1950s)		95.6	95.6 (1950s)	
Farms over 100 ha. as % of Total Farms		0.9			1.2			0.1	
Farms 1-10 ha. as % of Area Cultivated		32.3			14.5			74.3	
Farms over 100 ha. as % of Area Cultivated		39.0 (over 200 ha.)			13.1			7.7	
Average Annual Increase in Industrial Wages			8.4 (1964-8)			8.6 (1964-8)			10.8 (1964-8)
14. Inflation									
Consumer Price Level (1948 = 100)	100 (1948)	106 (1958)	137 (1967)	100 (1948)	147 (1958)	193 (1967)	100 (1948)	210 (1958)	254 (1967)
Average Annual Increase In Consumer Prices	0.9 (1951-60)	3.4 (1961-7)		3.8 (1951-60)	3.9 (1961-7)		5.8 (1951-60)	2.1 (1961-7)	

Sources:

1, 2, 8, 9, 10, 11, Irish and Greek data in 13, 14: IBRD, *World Tables* (Jan. 1971).

3, 4, 5, 6, 7: Banks *et al.* (1971).

12: U.S. Senate, Subcommittee of the Committee on Appropriations, 92nd Congress (1971: 72-73, 1260).

13: For Portugal: Carvalho (1969: 584-590). Land tenure data from J. F. Dewhurst, *et al.* (1961).

over Greece. As we saw in Table 7 this was less substantially the case in the late 1920s and early 1930s. In any case, during the 1950s and 1960s, these gaps tended to widen. While Greece was catching up on Ireland, Portugal fell further behind. Since its base was often inferior, occasionally Portugal's annual rate of per capita improvement was greater than that of its competitors. Obviously, this was the case for indicators which have a natural ceiling such as literacy, school enrolment and caloric intake.

In that 'classical' indicator of economic performance, per capita national income, Portugal appears to have lost ground relatively, especially with regard to Greece. Given differences in exchange rate policy, inflation and price controls over basic commodities, this may be a misleading finding. The Economic Commission for Europe, calculating per capita on the basis of regression analyses on physical commodities consumed about 1965, concluded that while Portugal's exchange-rated GNP per capita income was $405, Greece's $677 and Ireland's $943, the probable 'real' values were $733, $758 and $1239 respectively (see 'International Comparisons of Real Incomes', 1970: 139-152). This very substantially cuts down Greece's supposedly superior performance, while it hardly changes the relative position of Portugal and Ireland. The energy consumption index, perhaps a more reliable indicator of development, strongly supports the original observation that Greece has widened the gap. In fact, it started behind Portugal in 1950. Urbanization, literacy, secondary school and university enrolment and newspaper circulation also show Greece moving further ahead in the last decades. On all of these indicators Ireland had already attained levels in 1950 which Portugal was still far from reaching.

But the pattern of outcomes is not unequivocably embarrassing to Portugal. By the 1960s it was catching up in primary school enrolment, still had more radios and television sets per capita and consumed slightly more calories per person per day than Greece. Its imports and exports were more in balance; its accumulated international reserve holdings much greater and its rate of inflation far less than either of its 'competitors' – especially Greece, whose international trade account and internal pricing system looked very precarious. What may have permitted Greece to perform so well economically by comparison was the very substantial advantage it had in receiving so much economic and military aid from the United States. Portugal and Ireland were not so favored externally.

Finally, we come to the touchy question of income distribution. Consistent and comparable serial data by classes or percentile categories are not available, so we are forced to rely on an item in the national account statistics; the percentage of GNP paid out in wages and salaries.

Despite problems of comparability,[45] the data in row 13 of Table 14 show Ireland with a near 'developed European' pattern – over 60 per cent of GNP in wages and salaries. Portugal would appear to have had a more equal distribution of income than Greece, although the latter improved markedly from 1960 to 1968.

Since agriculture remains the economic activity of a substantial proportion of the population in all three countries (Portugal, 41.6 per cent; Ireland, 32.4 per cent; Greece, 54.7 per cent), land tenure is likely to have a strong impact on income distribution. The three countries had very different patterns. Both Portugal and Greece have a lot of *minifundistas* with less than 10 hectares. However, this group cultivates 74.3 per cent of the total farm land in Greece while the equivalent group in Portugal (89.9 per cent of the farms as opposed to 95.6 per cent in Greece) only farms 32.3 per cent of the cultivable surface. Looked at from the other end, those owning 0.9 per cent of the farms have 39.0 per cent of the area to work with. In Greece the top 0.7 per cent have only 7.7 per cent. The Irish pattern is dominated neither by *minifundismo* or *latifundismo,* but by medium-size independent farms. Certainly, in the case of Portugal, one can hardly make the *Estado Novo* responsible for such a highly unequal distribution of landed wealth, much of which developed long before its accession to power, although one can ask why it subsequently done nothing to change this situation and a good deal to sustain it.

Clearly, Caetano's boast that Portugal's workers have so painlessly obtained 'all the just benefits' of other European societies was (to put it politely) premature and (to put it realistically) increasingly less likely to happen. By virtually all of the usual standards of mass well-being, Portugal had slipped further behind. Globally speaking, the serial plot of such values for the 1950s and 1960s most closely approximates Figure 1c of Figure 1 and leads us to make a very negative evaluation of the output effort and outcome consequences of its type of authoritarian rule. This was perhaps not so surprising in relation to Ireland, but the Greek comparison was particularly damaging. There, despite high levels of political competitiveness and instability, large scale changes in levels of living and government services occurred which not only far surpassed those which took place in Portugal but brought Greece closer to the performance of developed European polities.

Nevertheless, Portugal's record was not entirely negative. Of course, one could argue that its citizenry have been spared the psychic anxiety of making political choices and the personal costs of suffering from disruptive social behaviour. Less obviously, its fiscally orthodox and economically conservative policies and its strong insistence on the decisional autonomy of state institutions, while they inhibited long-run growth and development, did produce a distributional outcome which appeared less unequal than that of Greece – but much more unequal than that of Ireland, or the rest of Europe for that matter. Greece's better general performance, accomplished with a heavy dose of state sponsorship, an unleashing of capitalist forces and substantial external support, resulted in enormous disparities in resources and returns. While the literature on Italian Fascism and German Naziism stresses the income concentration effect of such radical authoritarian regimes, (Pré, 1936 Rosenstock-Franck, 1934; Guerin, 1945), the Portuguese-Greek comparison suggests that capitalist development under stable, conservative authoritarian auspices may be less productive of inequality than under unstable, democratic auspices. This conclusion on outcomes, admittedly, is based on rather flimsy, cross-sectional data, a rather small margin of difference and largely overlooks the rural sector where concentration was much more marked in Portugal. It also overlooks the fact that Portugal's pattern of income distribution was not only much more skewed than that of developed Europe, but until very recently had shown no major redistributive trends.

CONCLUSION

> *Portuguese corporatism gives one the impression of an astonishing mixture of untruths and political vision. Always contradictory, its institutions are often founded 'in order not to exist', then exist 'in order not to function', finally one discovers that they have become consistent, but are not what they are said to be. Looking even closer, one suspects that this is more-or-less the way they were intended in the first place and that, therefore, the scheme is strong and at the same time ridiculous.* – Manuel Lucena

The temptation to dismiss Portuguese corporatism as having been both anachronistic and irrelevant is quite strong. In so doing, one would be echoing those who have already arrived at the conclusion that Mussolini's Corporative State was a mere 'confidence trick',[46] as well as those who insist on taking corporatism seriously as if it were a genuine *tertium genus* between capitalism and socialism. From either perspective, the practice of heretofore existing state sponsored corporatist institutions clearly has failed to live up to its ideological principles and promise. Hence, both could be dismissed as mere window-dressing of, at best, symbolic importance.

As Manuel Lucena's quote suggests, this contemptuous judgement may be both premature and naïve. Corporatist institutions may not have been designed, much less used, to accomplish such manifest goals. Nor may their actual performance be dismissed so easily as the unfortunate product of extraordinary circumstance and unintended consequence. They may not have done what their proponents say they wanted them to do and they may have been severely buffeted about by depression, war, imperialism and international competition, but this does not mean that they did not obey conscious (if unconfessed) purposes and perform important (if latent) functions.

At several points in this essay on Portugal and in previous work on Brazil, I have emphasized four aspects of the practice of state corporatism which seem to me crucial to understanding its relation, on the one hand, to social structure and, on the other hand, to public decision-making in an authoritarian political context.

The first is the extent to which 'sponsored' or state corporatism is *preemptive,* i.e. seeks to set out from above structures of associability and channels of interest representation in anticipation of spontaneous efforts by affected classes, sectors or groups. The second is the extent to which the corporatist experience is *preventive,* i.e. attempts not to mobilize or regiment its subjects for positive state-selected tasks but to ensure that normal or passive participation within its structures will occupy a certain physical, temporal and ideational 'space', foreclosing, if not prohibiting, alternative uses of that same space. The third is the extent to which such a mode of interest representation is *defensive,* i.e. encourages associations to act primarily, if not exclusively, in the protection of special corporate 'rights', privileges or exemptions granted from above, rather than in the 'aggressive' promotion of new projects or interests. The fourth is the extent to which it is *compartmental,* i.e. manages to confine potential conflicts within specialized, non-interacting decisional 'orders', thereby preventing the creation of multiple issue and multiple sector alliances or blocking 'partisan' appeals to wider publics and clientèles.

When one combines these four obviously interrelated dimensions, one is led to the conclusion that the role and consequences of state corporatism must be assessed, not primarily in terms of what it openly and positively accomplishes, but in terms of what it surreptitiously and negatively prevents from happening.

By doing so little positively and so much negatively, corporatism as practised in Portugal and other authoritarian regimes forged a durable set of asymmetric but reciprocal linkages or exchanges between subordinate groups who received differential functional pay-offs and protection from above, and superordinate authorities who received minimal information and some degree of voluntary compliance from below. Intervening in the relation between civil society and the state by deliberately and concertedly obfuscating the institutional distinction between these two realms of collective choice, corporatism functioned to prevent the emergence of obvious class hegemony or polarized group confontation, and the consequent loss of state autonomy which might otherwise have been produced as the result of capitalist development. As such, state corporatism was not the direct expression of a particular dominant social class or class alliance, but of a particular 'stalemated' configuration of social classes. Neither a *tertium genus* between capitalism and socialism, nor the product of atavistic 'feudal elites', nor the preferred outcome of 'monopoly capitalists',[47] corporatism in Portugal was, nevertheless, intimately related to the requirements of adjusting a system of political domination to the demands of capitalist accumulation and reproduction. Its enforced intra- and interclass 'harmony', coupled with its compartmentalization and bureaucratization of sectoral conflict, contributed immeasurably but significantly to establishing and sustaining the viability of such a pattern of gradual economic transformation on the periphery of the more autonomous and dynamic, i.e. 'liberal', centres of capitalist development. Its high total costs and skewed class incidence effects we have already noted in our comparison with Greece and Ireland.

It is, however, one thing to suggest the importance of state corporatism in having permitted Portugal to establish a particular type of political domination and economic exploitation during a particular developmental *conjoncture.*[48] It is quite another to speculate about corporatism's role once that *conjoncture* no longer exists.

And there is little doubt that the initial *conjoncture* has passed. Portugal's contemporary class structure is much more defined and consolidated. Its 'new' bourgeoisie seems to be chaffing at excessive bureaucratic regulation and the tutelary protection of inefficient producers (de Moura, 1968; 19; Lucena, 1971: vol. 1, 159). Certain of its sectors even seem willing and confident enough to participate in the more competitive arena of the European Economic Community and the 'Corporative Complex' is seen as preventing them from accomplishing this.[49] The working class also has become less artisan in origin and structure, and more conscious of its collective strength.[50] Even technical-professional *cadres* have begun to articulate 'modernizing' demands and to acquire some independent associational capacities.[51] Coupled with these longer-term structural changes are the more immediate problems associated with massive emigration, protracted colonial war, increased international competition and product substitution for its principal exports, heightened exposure to 'subversive' ideas through the diffusion of foreign mass media and the proliferation of foreign tourists. Even the Roman Catholic Church, heretofore such a firm legitimating element for both corporatism and authoritarian rule, began to withdraw its unconditional support (Cerqueira, 1973: 473-513). It seems that once again, as de Lampedusa's aristocrat says in *Il Gattopardo,* 'If things are going to stay the same around here, they will have to change'.

What fate awaited Portuguese corporatism in this new *conjoncture et structure* was not yet clear, although the Premier, Marcello Caetano, repeatedly gave assurances, not only that corporatism would be maintained, but that it would continue to be one of the main instruments of his projected 'renovation in continuity'.[52] What was at stake, therefore, was not 'liberalization' or the transformation of a corporatist system of interest representation into an open, autonomous, competitive pluralist one, but rather a calculated attempt at converting from one type of corporatism to another – from the involuntary, dependent, sponsored variety characteristic of authoritarian rule to the voluntaristic, interdependent and spontaneously evolved variety characteristic of the 'organized democracies' of advanced capitalist societies.

As one Portuguese scholar has pointed out, changes which appeared authoritarian when they occur elsewhere were perceived as liberating or even liberal when they occurred in Portugal (Pereira, 1971: 43). Western European and North American polities have steadily, if unself-consciously, evolved toward a form of 'societal' or spontaneous corporatism, particularly in the post-World War II period. Increased concentration in the structure and ownership of production, expansion in the planning and regulative role of state bureaucracies, wartime mobilization and rationing, pressure from international competition, decline in the salience of class-based ideologies, and growing acceptance of 'consumerist', privatistic goals are some of the major forces which have been cited as impelling this change.[53] These have, in turn, encouraged or accompanied a massive increase in the bureaucratization and concentration of power in singular, non-competitive interest associations, a noticeable decline in the relevance of territorially-based systems of representation such as parties and local governments, and a marked penetration of parliamentary and executive institutions by functionally specified organized interests. The 'liberal-pluralist' distinction between public and private decisional arenas, between civil society and the state, has consequently weakened, if not disappeared. Ironically, this spontaneous and unselfconscious evolution[54] toward a system where interest associations have

> a quasi-legal status, and a prescriptive right to speak for their segment of the population influence the process of government directly, by-passing the Diet . . deputize for the State in whole sectors of public life, and . . . have duties delegated to them that properly belong to the civil service (Huntford, 1971: 86)[55]

is much closer in practice to the principles enunciated by corporatist ideologues than the self-conscious and self-confessed attempts to implement these same principles from above.

Simply because contemporary, 'organized democracies' with their welfare state and managed economies, had demonstrated that formerly competitive, multiple, overlapping, i.e. pluralist, interest systems can develop (one is tempted to say, decay) into a form of societal corporatism was, of course, no guarantee that Portugal would be able to revivify its stalemated state corporatist system. The societal corporatist outcome seems to depend on its own liberal-pluralist origins – on a history of autonomous organizational development, authentic representational efforts, protracted encounters between classes and sectors which acquired distinctive self-images and associational loyalties and, eventually, a measure of mutual respect; on the simultaneous presence of a competitive party and parliamentary system to which wider public appeals could be addressed; and, perhaps most importantly, on a previous pattern of relative non-interference by the state which only gradually came to expand its policy scope and to participate in inter-associational struggles – usually at the request of organized 'private' interests. Countries such as Portugal, following a very different trajectory, have found it much more difficult to evolve toward such a consensual solution. There the history was one of asymmetric dependence, unauthentic and fragmented representation, suppressed and manipulated conflicts, weak associational loyalties, little mutual respect between groups, no effective means of appealing to wider publics, and pervasive state bureaucratic control. Granted that Portugal's self-proclaimedly reformist but still authoritarian leaders would have liked (and perhaps badly needed) the sort of reliable information, stabilizing intermediate loyalties and collaboration which societal corporatism could provide, but the timidity, uncertainty and inconsistency which marked their efforts to 'modernize' Portugal's representational system and its public policy-making structures suggest that they were far from being able to form their compulsory *estado corporativo* into a consensual *estado social.*

A SHORT EPILOGUE

Since this essay was written, a *coup* by junior military officers abruptly and unexpectedly liberated Portugal from authoritarian rule. While at present (December 1974) it is still not clear whether this event and the processes unleashed by it will have revolutionary consequences for the country's economic and social structures, it has already had an irreversible impact upon its political institutions.

Virtually the entire 'Corporative complex' described in this monograph was dissolved almost overnight, initially by popular action and subsequently by official decree. It collapsed almost without resistance, along with the other pillars of Portuguese authoritarian rule: the government party, the youth group, the para-military Legião, the various police and intelligence apparatuses, etc. Since April, 1974 it has been replaced by a veritable 'beehive' of autonomous, voluntaristic, competitive, overlapping, non-hierarchic associational activity. Portugal has suddenly become one of the most pluralistic polities in existence, and there are at least preliminary indications, in the form of a proposed 'syndical law', that its present rulers intend to encourage it to stay that way.

Pending a more detailed and comprehensive analysis of 'liberated Portugal' (in which I am currently engaged), one might advance briefly several 'lessons' with respect specifically to corporatism:

1) Portugal's previous corporative institutions were even more weak and sclerotic, unrepresentative and unpopular than my essay depicted them. They never had any chance of surviving even an ambiguous change at the top executive level of the political system.

2) The fraudulence of the alleged 'congruence' between corporatism and Portugal's political culture was revealed for all to see. Given just the suggestion of a choice, the population massively and spontaneously 'elected' a different system of interest representation. As one Swiss observer put it:

> The Portuguese national temperament has often been described as passive, fatalistic and endlessly melancholy. But anyone travelling through Portugal these days cannot help wondering to what extent this supposed 'temperament' was not imposed by 48 years of police-state atmosphere.

3) Corporatism, itself, did not contribute directly to the collapse of authoritarian rule. Rather, it was what it had earlier prevented from occurring – the spread of rationalistic technocratic reform within the state apparatus and the extension of some modicum of authentic representational accountability – that led indirectly to undermining the legitimacy and capacity to resist of the Portuguese state, when faced with a profound crisis in its civil-military relations. When 'push came to shove', there were no dedicated corporative cadres to defend the *ancien régime.*

4) Finally, the Portuguese case strongly supports the assertion that there exists no linear, continuous process whereby imposed state corporatism can transform itself into consensual societal corporatism. Some form of open, competitive even combative, interest politics – pluralism in other words – must intercede before authoritarian polities such as Portugal can expect to reach the haven of 'organized democracy'.

NOTES

1. For example, on the United States, see Lowi (1969) and McConnell (1966); on the Netherlands: Kraemer (1966); on Sweden: Huntford (1971). Of special relevance is the study by Harris (1972: 62-74) of postwar British policy-making.

2. I have discussed these divergent-convergent routes to 'state' and 'societal' corporatism at some length in Schmitter (1974: 85-131).

3. For the hint that this might be the case in one of Europe's most consistently democratic systems, see Rokkan (1966: 70-115). See also Schmitter (1974).

4. Durkheim (1964: 1-31) is perhaps the best known essay from this *solidariste* position. Elbow (1953: 97-121) contains a historical exposition of this current of French thought.

5. Draper (1961: 87-106) discusses the left-wing intellectual origins of corporatism and related, more recent, liberal North American writings on the political role of corporations: Burnham, Berle, Buchanan, Drucker, Mason and Ferry. Also Halevy (1965: 265-316).

6. For example, where does one place J. M. Keynes' advocacy of a return to 'medieval conceptions of separate autonomies' and 'corporations (acting as) a mode of government' in Keynes (1931: 317-319)?

7. Salazar's public speeches have been collected in a six-volume series. Of particular interest is the first which covers the formative period of the corporative system (Salazar, 1961).

8. Nevertheless, even one of Portugal's most enthusiastic corporatists concluded that 'contrary to what happened in the countries of northern and central Europe, the [medieval] Portuguese corporations never attained a high degree of economic and social power' (Caetano, 1935: 37).

9. See Quieró (1961: 43). Nevertheless, the International Labour Organization in its 1928 survey, *Freedom of Association,* Vol. IV (Geneva: ILO, 1928: 296)

concluded: 'It may be said that the whole existence of the trade associations [in Portugal] from the moment of their constitution . . . to that of their dissolution . . . is dependent on the executive authorities'. In short, the practice and precedent of state control over associability definitely antedate the *Estado Novo.* It, however, will add the element of sponsorship and subsidization from above and greatly expand the number and variety of control mechanisms.

10. International comparisons of association formation are difficult to make given wide disparities in registration procedures and non-equivalences in territorial scope. Nevertheless, Juan Linz reports that in 1933 Spain had 10,479 worker and 4,642 employer associations. In 1934 Portugal had 754 and 285 respectively, plus some 37 'mixed ones'. At the time Spain's population was roughly 4½ to 5 times that of Portugal. Using the upper-bound estimate, this would indicate that Spain had proportionately 2.7 times as many workers' associations and over three times as many employers' associations. See also Linz (1971: 307-348).

11. Speech of 30 July 1930 (See Salazar, 1961: Vol. I: 67-96).

12. Caetano (1935: 12 and 1938: 27-32) who was one of the original architects of the *Estado Novo,* has personally testified to the influence of *integralista* ideology along with the Social Christian inspiration, Italian fascist practice and French solidarist-legal doctrines in the construction of Portuguese corporatism. For a more detailed treatment of *integralismo* and subsequently derived nationalist-authoritarian-fascist movements, see Martins (1968: 302-336). Also Proenca (1964) and Ferrão (1964).

13. Caetano (1935) contains an extensive treatment of Mussolini's scheme and abundant citations from Italian corporatist theorists. Nevertheless, he and other Portuguese exponents sharply differentiated their 'pure corporatism' from the 'subordinated or state corporatism' of Mussolini, relying on a distinction pioneered by Manoïlesco. The actual practice of Portuguese corporatism, as we shall see, was much closer to its Italian forerunner.

14. For example, a leading Portuguese theorist of corporatism in congratulating Salazar on his 'absolutely scientific . . . [and] eminently practical' orientation could claim that the *Estado Novo* was the embodiment of principles advocated by 'notable thinkers of diverse schools': Saint-Simon, Sismondi, La Tour du Pin, Leo XIII, Pius X and Pius XI, Georges Valois, Emile Durkheim, Leon Duguit, 'the whole syndicalist school' – and, of course, Mussolini! (See Gonçalves, 1936).

15. An important primary source for public policy during this early period is the annual budget reports drafted personally by Salazar. These have been conveniently compiled in *Doze Anos na Pasta das Finanças.* 1928-1940.

16. While in retrospect the transition from military dictatorship to civilian authoritarian rule appears to have passed smoothly, during the event there was a considerable amount of uncertainty, tension and resistance (but see also Martins, 1968). The standard, eulogistic treatments needless to say, play down such elements – as well as the use of coercion – e.g. Derrick (1939); Egerton (1943), Mayer (1939); Ferro (1939) D'Assac (1967: 72) adds a nice touch when, admitting the uncertainty and violence of the 1930-33 period, he attributes responsibility for it to a Masonic plot; also de Poncins (1936).

17. The extraordinary legal and procedural complexity of the Portuguese corporatist system is brilliantly analyzed in Lucena (1971). Thanks to Sr. Lucena I was able to consult his unpublished dissertation in the course of my research and it has contributed both substantively and theoretically a great deal to my understanding

of corporatism's role, especially in its relation to Portuguese social and economic structure.

18. It should, however, be recalled that the régime simultaneously and forcibly closed down and seized the property of some 754 workers' associations.

19. Cf. III Colòquio Nacional do Trabalho da Organizaçao Corporativa e da Previdência Social, Comunicaçoes e Conclusóes (Lisbon, 1964), pp. 105 ff. for a very extensive treatment of the problem of the small size and scope and very weak financial base of the National Syndicates.

20. Partial biographical data on rural representatives in the Corporative Chamber indicates that it was by no means uncommon for the same man to have been head of both the Casa do Povo and the Grémio da Lavoura in a given locality.

21. In fact, the government directly appoints members of the Grémio's governing council (Lucena, 1971, Vol. I: 152).

22. This shift from Grémios Obrigatórios to Organismos do Coordenaçao Econômica is treated in some detail in Cotta. Cotta (1937: 107) concludes: 'The government in organizing production, processing and distributing separately, simply took things as they were, creating as little disturbance as possible and respecting all interests as long as they were not incompatible with the public good'.

23. Lest one infer from the survival of these 'private' representative associations the existence of a strong resistance to authoritarian rule or state corporatism on the part of liberal industrialists and merchants, I offer the following quote from Caetano (1956: 180) 'Almost a quarter of a century of corporative organization . . . did not manage to destroy the Industrial and Commercial Associations. [Was this] due to the spirit of resistance on the part of its members and leaders to the new order? I know positively not, since at the head of these associations have been some of the elements most devoted to the Estado Novo and some to whom are owed great favors'.

24. The Corporative Council is a governmental, not a representative, body which formally oversees the operation of the whole corporative system. It used to be composed of the major ministries plus the President of the Council and two law school professors. The professors and some of the ministers were dropped in 1955. Since 1960, the elected presidents of Corporaçoes have obtained some access to it.

25. Its appointed president is always a naval officer, the Captain of the Port in which the Casa is located.

26. See Lopez-Cardoso (1968) for an extensive discussion of the relation between rural interest representation, the land tenure system and agricultural productivity.

27. The União Nacional (UN) was created years after the seizure of power and shortly *before* the new constitution was announced in 1933. An improvisation, the UN did not emerge from any prior movement or party, although it did co-opt many of the fascist 'National Syndicalists' and some of the monarchists – its principle partisan competitors of the time. The UN rarely held congresses and made no effort at mass recruitment. Salazar himself was opposed to all parties and declared: 'We shall not allow parties to form . . . It was on purpose to amalgamate everybody of political activity which might show itself that the National Union was formed. . . Membership (in) the National Union, for instance, will be no substitute for real competence; nor will a member take preference over any hard-working, loyal, and competent but non-affiliated civil servant . . .' (Ferro, 1939: 145-146). In short, the UN was a deliberate non-party, created to occupy political space and structure the formal electoral process, but not to exert a monopoly on ideological diffusion or recruitment to authoritative positions. Recently the UN was renamed, Açao Nacional

Popular, and institutionally reinvigorated. A series of local commissions were created and instructed to 'organize cadres, indoctrinate them and attempt to arrive, through them, to the masses'. Nevertheless, ANP's statutes insisted that it was a 'civic association', (which) 'has no partisan character nor feeds the partisan spirit'.

28. 'The corporative organization was intended . . . as a process designed to remove *(descongestionar)* in the future many of the functions of the state . . . through self-discipline . . . . [Due to the war] there came a hardening of structures, characterized by a greater centralization of powers which corresponded to a weakening of the autonomy of the organs of economic coordination and the institutions of corporatism themselves and to a reinforcing of authoritarianism, leavi the private sector without the participation and collaboration which had been intended . . . . The end of the war did not permit an immediate economic demobilization; neither did the Administration show itself very disposed to renounce so easily the preponderance it had acquired' (Caetano, 1966: 260-261; also Caetano, no date: 115-142).

29. Membership data on employer Grémios were not consistently available for the whole period, but its addition, while it would almost double the total, would not alter the strong evidence of numerical stagnation in the late 1940s and 1950s.

30. For example, this same source discloses that the total income of the Corporations in 1968-69 varied from $163,000 (Industry) to $12,000 (Entertainment), hardly enough to conduct large scale promotional campaigns and independent research. (As Corporações na Economia Nacional, 1971: 173 ff.)

31. For example, although Corporation presidents are elected 'autonomously' by employers' and workers' representatives, the government directly appoints 'observers' to the governing council and these are empowered to attend all meetings, consult all documents, veto all proposals and halt all deliberations when, in their judgement, 'there is need for enlightenment on the orientation to follow'. This is an arrangement similar to that used in the original Grémios Obrigatórios in 1933. (Lucena, 1971, Vol. I: 186-192).

32. I am basing this assessment on Cutileiro (1971) and conversations with Joyce Riegelhaupt, emphasizing the political impotence of local communities.

33. For a comprehensive description of this complex 'dual presidential' system, see dos Santos, (1940). Subsequent constitutional changes are discussed in Carneiro (1971). For differing perspectives on this crucial 1958 election see Kay, (1970: 341-356) and Fryer and Pinheiro, (1963: 93-96).

34. In an excellent newspaper article, a Brazilian journalist analyzed the conflicts over the renomination of Admiral Américo Thomaz to the presidency of the republic. According to his account, all the contending candidacies and most of the manoeuvring groups came from factions within the armed forces. No mention was made of the Acao Nacional Popular, except in passively approving Thomaz's candidacy. (Almada, 1972). Howe (1972) disclosed that Caetano desisted from presenting himself as candidate due to a military veto.

35. These opinions have been regularly compiled since 1935 in an annual volume, Pareceres de Câmara Corporativa, which is both a principal source for the following the functioning of the Chamber and an indispensible source of primary data for the functioning of the system as a whole since the pareceres often provide historical and factual material not available elsewhere. For the observation that these opinions are 'searching' and 'by no means without influence', see Kay, (1970: 77).

36. I am deeply indebted to Dr. Manuel Cabeçadas Ataïde for having made available to me his collection of 3" x 5" cards on members of the Legislative Assembly and Corporative Chamber from 1935 to 1967. The tabulations presented herein should be considered tentative as they have been visually interpreted and manually sorted. In the future I hope to have these data coded and machine-processed which will also permit a more extensive analysis of career patterns. The original source of the data is the biographical sketches found in República Portuguesa, Anais da Assembléia Nacional e da Camara Corporativa, (Lisboa: Assembléia Nacional, 1935-1970).

37. For some revealing comments on the operation of the Câmara – i.e. the technical nature of its work, the dominant role of its sectorally differentiated, permanent subcommittees, the unanimity of its decisional process, see Cardoso (1958: 121, 140-150).

38. Admittedly, some defenders of the Estado Novo would deny the validity of any matched comparison with another polity on grounds of the (imagined) unparallelled magnitude of political instability under the Republic and/or the unique peculiarities of Portuguese culture and history.

39. Nevertheless, Ireland has harboured in its midst a revolutionary party, the Sinn Fein, and a para-military organization, the Irish Republican Army. These were especially active in the 1930s, as was a proto-fascist Army Comrades Association (the Blue-shirts) (Chubb, 1970: 71-72, 89).

40. For a discussion of the methodological and inferential issues raised by this type of research design (and the inspiration for my utilizing it), see Campbell and Stanley, (1966); also Campbell, (1970: 110-125).

41. Actually a comprehensive evaluation of policy performance should disaggregate the welfare indicators by class and perhaps region. Absolute or per capita increases for the unit as a whole may, of course, disguise important concentration effects. Much of the literature in support of democratic rule emphasizes its presumed egalitarian distributional impact on economic and social welfare; authoritarian apologists tend to emphasize general system performance. In this sense, by using indicators of the latter we are (once again) meeting the regime's proponents on their preferred grounds.

42. Banks (1971) is a major step in this direction and I have made extensive use of it. However, it suffers from excessive reliance on linearly interpolated yearly values and absence of relevant policy output and outcome indicators.

43. Chubb (1970: 95-120), in an extensive description of Irish interest groups notes the 'absence of powerful and active corporate institutions' and concludes that 'like industry, labor is not very well organized', (107). He also gives substantially lower figures on trade union membership, the total being complicated by the territorial demarcation between Northern and Republican Ireland.

44. Data on strikes in Portugal are needless to say, not available, although strikes and worker demonstrations were not infrequent. An opposition newsletter published in London, the Portuguese and Colonial Bulletin, did carry extensive and numerous accounts of work stoppages but it is difficult to assess its reliability or to code it for comparative purposes. Nevertheless, the Bulletin was a major and important antidote to the bland, compliant and censored press within the country at that time.

45. The Portuguese government did not provide data on wages as a percentage of GNP, as do all other OECD members. The Portuguese data, displayed in Table 14 are estimates by economists. See Carvalho (1969: 584-590). Compare Pré (1936) and Rosenstock-Franck (1934); also Querin (1945).

46. Times Literary Supplement (1 March 1973) as cited in Newton (1973).

47. Lucena (1971) has very subtly analyzed this issue of the class basis of Portuguese corporatism: 'The state, in the course of this (evolutionary) process, dealt with capitalists with a velvet but heavy hand. Using capitalism, it remained ahead (but not brilliantly) of most capitalists. It assisted the most powerful, but it also obstructed them. It captured all of them, (large and small) in the thickest of regulatory nets. Finally, it is itself a large entrepreneur, against the wishes of its founder, but in agreement with the imperative laws of the economic system', (Vol. 1, 56); 'One must never forget that, especially in its beginnings, this (corporatist) system was a creature of the state. It was not created by the dominant class, which had to be carefully reassured', (Vol. 1, 75 bis); 'Portuguese corporatism controls the sphere of labor without, however, obeying that of capital. It is the state which created *de toutes pièces* their forced agreement which has benefited capital. The latter had neither unity nor clear ideas. And, it does not always show itself properly appreciative', (Vol. I, 126); 'The New State has been the avant garde of a bourgeoisie that did not support it' (Vol. II, 292).

48. This is not to argue with Marx that corporatist-authoritarian rule 'was the only form of government possible at a time when the bourgeoisie had already lost, and the working class had not yet acquired, the faculty of ruling the nation' (Civil War in France, 56). More pertinent might be the hypothesis that such a regime configuration becomes even more likely when neither class had yet acquired the ability to rule, but the transition from the pre-capitalist to capitalist mode of production was imposed upon the nation from without.

49. This emerges clearly from data gathered by Harry Makler on a national sample of Portuguese industrialists. Professor Makler and I are currently analyzing this in an essay tentatively entitled: 'Portugal Faces the European Economic Community'.

50. Here the evidence is more difficult to obtain, but the formation (and suppression) of 'intersyndical commissions' across sectors of the working class and scattered reports of strikes, work stoppages and slow-downs especially among metallurgical workers, bank and clerical employees points in the direction of greater class consciousness and collective activity.

51. Here the principal innovation was the creation of SEDES, an independent 'civil association' composed of younger técnicos, lawyers and journalists as well as the activity of some of its members and/or sympatisants in administrative positions within the former regime.

52. See especially Caetano (1968 and 1970). As recently as 1973 Caetano claimed that 'the Corporative State has the qualities to continue to put into practice all that socialist parties have proposed to do in the countries where they exist. The corporative lesson remains worthy and up-to-date'.

53. This theme of the 'corporatization' of the interest systems of advanced industrial societies has been given a preliminary exploration in works cited above. For the specific delineation of factors behind this transformation in Western Europe as well as a discussion of the prospects for a change in the type of corporatism in Portugal, I am especially indebted to Lucena (1971). The difference in developmental pattern between 'state' and 'societal' corporatism and the relation of both to capitalist development I have explored in my 'Still the Century of Corporatism? ' essay (1974).

54. Pinto gleefully refers to this as 'unconfessed corporatism'. See Pinto (1955, Vol. I: 40-81) for an extensive catalogue of such practices in Western developed politics.

55. Sweden may well be the most advanced case of societal corporatism – even discounting for the exaggerated elements in Huntford's argument – but it is not far ahead of such polities as the Netherlands, Norway, Switzerland and Austria. Even more fascinating is the way in which this emergent pattern is imposing itself at all levels of decision-making from the various attempts at institutionalized 'participation' in individual firms, through the Comités Economiques et Sociaux attached to the recently created French Regional Councils, and finally, to the European Economic Community which has institutionalized corporatism on a supra-national scale. Self-described corporatist states have been by no means as thorough in replicating its forms and practices. Portugal, for example, never extended its scope to cover the 'overseas provinces', nor tolerated any participatory 'co-gestion' at the level of individual firms or even economic sectors.

REFERENCES

ALLEMANN, F. R. (1969) 'Portugal no Caminho do Século XX': Cadernos Brasileiros, No. 54 (July-August).

ANDERSON, C. W. (1970) The Political Economy of Modern Spain. Madison and London: University of Wisconsin Press.

AS CORPORAÇOES NA ECONOMIA NACIONAL (1971) Lisbon: Corporação do Comercio.

AZPAIZU, J. J. (1951) The Corporative State. St. Louis and London: B. Herder.

BACHELOR, L. W. (1973) "Corporatism and Parliamentary Politics in the Second French Republic". M.A. paper. University of Chicago.

BANKS, A. S. (1972) updated printout of Cross-Polity Time-Series Data.

BANKS, et al. (1971) Cross-Polity Time-Series Data. Cambridge, Massachusetts and London: MIT Press.

CAETANO, M. (no date) Paginas Inoportunas. Lisbon: Livraria Bertrand.

CAETANO, M. (1973) Le Monde Diplomatique. (August).

CAETANO, M. (1970) 'Estado Social.' Excerpts published by the Secretaria de Estado da Informaçao e Turismo.

CAETANO, M. (1968) 'Corporative Revolution, Permanent Revolution'. Speeches reprinted as a pamphlet of the Secretaria de Estado da Informaçao e Turismo.

CAETANO, M. (1966) 'Problemas Actuales de la Administración Pública Portuguesa'. Documentación Administrativa No. 100 (April). Madrid.

CAETANO, M. (1956) 'Uma Experiencia Politica bem Sucedida: O Estado Novo Português'. IV Congresso da União Nacional. Sessões Plenarias. Lisbon.

CAETANO, M. (1938) O Sistema Corporativo. Lisbon: O Jornal do Comércio.

CAETANO, M. (1935) Lições de Direito Corporativo. Lisbon: Oficina Gráfica.

CAMPBELL, D. T. (1970) 'The Connecticut Crackdown on Speeding: Time-Series Data on Quasi-Experimental Analysis' in E. R. Tufts (ed.) The Quantitative Analysis of Social Problems. Reading, Massachusetts: Addison-Wesley.

CAMPBELL, D. T. and J. C. STANLEY (1966) Experimental and Quasi-Experimental Designs for Research. Chicago: Rand McNally.
CARDOSO, J. P. (1958) Questões Corporativas, Doutrina e Factos, Lisbon: Gabinete de Estudos Corporativos.
CARNEIRO, F. S. (1971) As Revisões da Constituição Política de 1933. Porto: Brasília Editora.
CERQUEIRA, S. (1973) 'L'Eglise Catholique et la Dictature Corporatiste Portugaise'. Revue Française de Science Politique. Volume XXIII, No. 3 (June).
CHUBB, B. (1970) The Government and Politics of Ireland. Stanford: University Press.
CLARK, C. (1957) The Conditions of Economic Progress (3rd ed). London: Macmillan.
COSTA JUNIOR (1964) Historia Breve do Movimiento Operario Português. Lisbon: Editorial Verbo.
COTTA, F. (1937) Economic Planning in Corporative Portugal. London: P. S. King.
CUTILEIRO, J. (1971) A Portuguese Rural Society. Oxford: The Clarendon Press.
D'ASSAC, J. P. (1967) Salazar, Paris: La Table Ronde.
DA FONSECA, J. R. (1934) Cem Anos em Defesa da Economia Nacional, 1834-1934. Lisbon: Associação Comercial de Lisboa.
DE ALMADA, J. (1972) 'Reeleição de Thomaz Descontentou Generais'. O Estado de São Paulo (30 July).
DE CARVALHO, O. E. (1969) 'Aspectos de Repartição do Rendimento em Portugal.' Análise Social, Volume VII, No. 27-28.
DE LA SOUCHERE, E. (1970) 'Portugal. Caetano's Ambiguous Reforms.' Le Monde: Weekly Selection (18 February).
DE MOURA, F. P. (1968) Por Onde Vai a Economia Portuguesa? Lisbon: Seará Nova.
DE PONCINS, L. (1936) Le Portugal Renaît Paris: G. Beauchesne.
DERRICK, M. (1939) The Portugal of Salazar. New York: Campion Books.
DEWHURST, J. F. et al. (1961) Europe's Needs and Resources. New York: Twentieth Century Fund.
DOS SANTOS, F. I. P. (1940) Un Etat Corporative. La Constitution Sociale et Politique Portugaise (2nd ed.). Paris: Librairie du Recueil Sirey.
DOZE ANOS NA PASTA DAS FINANÇAS, 1928-1940 (1968) (2 volumes). Lisbon: Corporacao do Comercio.
DRAPER, H. (1961) 'Neo-Corporatists and Neo-Reformers.' New Politics, Vol. 1, No. 1 (Autumn).
DURKHEIM, E. (1964) The Division of Labor in Society. New York: The Free Press.
EASTON, D. (1965) A Systems Analysis of Political Life. New York: John Wiley.
THE ECONOMIST (1968): 'Half a Liberal is Better than None', (anon.), 2 November.
EGERTON, F. C. C. (1943) Salazar, Rebuilder of Portugal. London: Hodder and Stoughton.
ELBOW, M. H. (1953) French Corporative Theory, 1789-1948: New York: Columbia University Press.
FERRÃO, C. (1964) O Integralismo e a República. Lisbon: Inquérito.
FERRO, A. (1939) Salazar, Portugal and her Leader. London: Faber & Faber.
FRYER, P. and P. M. PINHEIRO (1963) Le Portugal de Salazar. Paris: Ruedo Ibérico.

GARNIER, C. (1952) Vacances avec Salazar. Paris: B. Grasset.
GONÇALVES, L. DA C. (1936) Causas e Efeitos do Corporativismo Portugues. Lisbon: Instituto Superior de Ciencias Económicas e Financeiras.
GUERIN, D. (1945) Fascisme et Grand Capital (2nd ed.) Paris: Gallimard.
HALEVY, E. (1965) The Era of Tyrannies: New York: Anchor Books.
HARRIS, N. (1972) Competition and the Corporate Society. London: Methuen.
HOWE, M. (1972) 'Portuguese Find the Spirit of Salazar Still Dominant.' The New York Times (20 August).
HUNTFORD, R. (1971) The New Totalitarians. London: Allen Lane.
IBRD, World Tables (January 1971).
ILO, Yearbook (appropriate years). (Geneva: International Labour Organization).
'INTERNATIONAL COMPARISONS OF REAL INCOMES, CAPITAL FORMATION AND CONSUMPTION' (1970). Economic Survey of Europe. New York: UN, ECE.
JACOB, H. and M. LIPSKY (1971) "Outputs, Structure and Power: An Assessment of Changes in the Study of State and Local Politics" in R. Hofferbert and I. Sharkansky (eds.) State and Urban Politics: Readings in Comparative Public Policy. Boston: Little, Brown & Co.
JECCHINIS, C. (1967) Trade Unionism in Greece. Chicago: Roosevelt University, Labor Education Division.
KAY, H. (1970) Salazar and Modern Portugal. London: Eyre and Spottiswoode.
KENNEDY, K. A. (1971) Productivity and Industrial Growth. Oxford: The Clarendon Press.
KEESING'S CONTEMPORARY ARCHIVES (appropriate years).
KEYNES, J. M. (1931) "The End of Laissez-Faire". Essays in Persuasion. London: Macmillan.
KRAEMER, P. E. (1966) The Societal State. Meppel: Boom en Zoon.
LEGG, K. (1969) Politics in Modern Greece. Stanford: Stanford University Press.
LEITE, J. P. DE C. (1936) A Doctrina Corporativa em Portugal. Lisbon: Livraria Clássica.
LINZ, J. (1971) 'La Realidad Associativa de los Espanoles'. Sociología Espanola de los Anos Setenta. Madrid: Confederación Espanola de Cajas de Ahorros.
LINZ, J. (1970) 'An Authoritarian Regime: Spain' in E. Allardt and S. Rokkan (eds.) Mass Politics. New York: The Free Press.
LOPEZ-CARDOSO, A. (1968) 'Le Portugal. Structures Agraires et Système Politique Analyse et Prévision', Volume VI, No. 6.
LOWI, T. J. (1969) The End of Liberalism. New York: W. W. Norton.
LUCENA, M. (1971) L'Evolution du Système Corporatif Portugais à Travers les Lois (1933-1971). 2 Volumes. Paris: Institut des Sciences Sociales du Travail.
McCONNELL, G. (1966) Private Power of American Democracy. New York: Knopf.
MANOILESCO, M. (1934) Le Siècle du Corporatisme. Paris: Felix Alcan.
MARTINS, H. (1968) 'Portugal' in S. J. Woolf (ed.) European Fascism. London: Weidenfeld and Nicolson.
MAYER, A. (1939) Portugal und Sein Weg Zum Autoritären Staat. Leipzig: Goldmann.
MEYNAUD, J. (1965) Les Forces Politiques en Grece. Lausanne: Etudes de Science Politique.
NEWTON, R. (1973) 'The Corporate Idea and the Authoritarian Tradition in Spain and Spanish America: Some Critical Observations'. Paper presented at the LASA Congress. Madison, Wisconsin.

NUNES, A. S. (1954) Situação e Problemas do Corporativismo. Lisbon: Gabinete de Estudos Corporativos.
PACHECO, J. (1971) As Lutas Operarias Contra a Carestia de Vida em Portugal. A Greve de Novembro de 1918. Lisbon: Portucalense Editôra.
PARECERES DA CÂMARA CORPORATIVA.
PEP, European Political Parties (1970), New York: Praeger.
PEREIRA, J. M. (1971) Pensar Portugal Hoje. Lisbon: Dom Quixote.
PEREIRA, P. T. (1937) A Batalha do Futuro (2nd ed.) Lisbon: Livraria Clássica.
PINTO, J. M. C. (1955) A Corporação (2 volumes). Coimbra: Coimbra Editora.
PIROU, G. (1939) Néo-Libéralisme, Néo-Corporatisme, Néo-Socialisme. Paris: Gallimard.
PIROU, G. (1938) Essais sur le Corporatisme. Paris: Librairie du Recueil Sirey.
PORTUGAL, ANUARIO ESTATISTICO (various editions).
PRE, R. (1936) L'Organisation des Rapports Economiques et Sociaux dans les Pays à Regime Corporatiste. Paris: Librarie Technique et Economique.
PROENÇA, R. (1964) Acerca do Integralismo Lusitano. Lisbon: Seará Nova.
QUIERÓ, A. R. (1961) 'O Estatuto do Trabalho Nacional Antes de 1930'. 1º Colóquio Nacional do Trabalho da Organização Corporativa e da Previdência Social. Sessões Plenarias. Lisbon.
REPÚBLICA PORTUGUESA, Ministério das Finanças, Annuário Estatístico de Portugal, 1921. Lisbon: Imprensa Nacional, 1925.
ROKKAN, S. (1966) 'Norway: Numerical Democracy and Corporate Pluralism' in R. Dahl (ed.) Political Oppositions in Western Democracies. New Haven and London: Yale University Press.
ROSENSTOCK-FRANCK, L. (1934) L'Economie Corporative Fasciste en Doctrine et en Fait. Paris: Camber.
RUDEL, C. (1968) Le Portugal et Salazar. Paris: Editions Ouvrières.
SALAZAR, O. (1961) Discursos (5th ed. revised). Coimbra: Coimbra Editora.
SARTI, R. (1971) Fascism and Industrial Leadership in Italy, 1919-1940. Berkeley, Los Angeles and London: University of California Press.
SCHMITTER, P. C. (1974) 'Still the Century of Corporatism? ' in F. Pike and T. Stritch (eds.) The New Corporatism. Notre Dame and London: University of Notre Dame Press.
SCHMITTER, P. C. (1972a) 'Paths to Political Development in Latin America'. Proceedings of the American Academy of Political Science, Volume 30, No. 4.
SCHMITTER, P. C. (1972b) 'The Comparative Analysis of Public Policy: Outputs, Outcomes and Impacts'. Paper for the SSRC Conference on the Comparative Analysis of Public Policy Performances (25-28 January). Princeton, New Jersey.
SCHMITTER, P. C. (1971) Interest Conflict and Political Change in Brazil. Stanford: Stanford University Press.
SILVA, J. (1971) Memorias de um Operário. Porto: Livraria Julião Brandão.
TEIXEIRA, A. B. (1961) 'O Pensamento Associacionista e Corporativo en Portugal no Século XIX' in 1º Colóquio Nacional do Trabalho da Organização Corporativa e da Previdência Social. Communicações, Vol. 3. Lisbon.
UNESCO, World Illiteracy at Mid-Century (1967) Paris: UNESCO.
U.S. Senate, Sub-committee of the Committee on Appropriations, 92nd Congress (1971). Foreign Assistance and Related Programs Appropriations. Washington, DC: GPO.
VIEIRA, A. (1970) Para a Historia do Sindicalismo em Portugal. Porto: Seará Nova.
VIEIRA, A. (1950) Em Volta da Minha Professão. Lisbon: Edição do Autor.

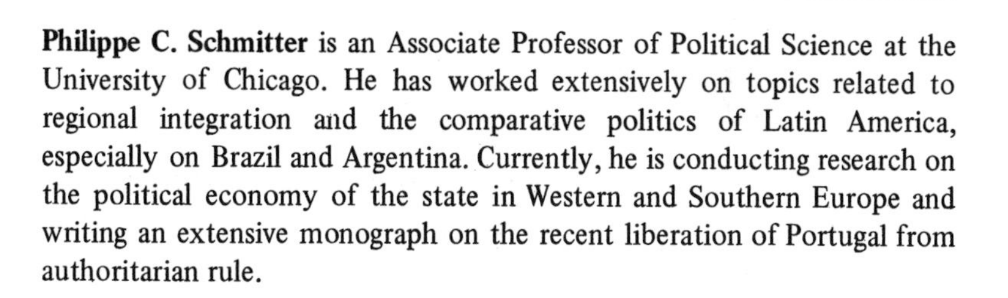

Philippe C. Schmitter is an Associate Professor of Political Science at the University of Chicago. He has worked extensively on topics related to regional integration and the comparative politics of Latin America, especially on Brazil and Argentina. Currently, he is conducting research on the political economy of the state in Western and Southern Europe and writing an extensive monograph on the recent liberation of Portugal from authoritarian rule.

Sage Library of Social Research

The work of many prominent social scientists – in writing, research, analysis and synthesis – is of interest and importance far beyond the boundaries of traditional disciplines and sub-fields. It is to present such works – diverse in subject and in audience – that the SAGE LIBRARY OF SOCIAL RESEARCH has been created.

NATIONAL CONSCIOUSNESS IN DIVIDED GERMANY

Gebhard Ludwig Schweigler

Introduction by Karl Deutsch **Volume 15**

How many German peoples are there today – one or two? How many German nations are there today – one or two? How many stable German States? Dr Schweigler brings together cultural, literary and sociological research to create a scholarly framework for the study of these questions, and suggests some practical analyses which result. The book focuses on national consciousness as an analytical concept, on trend analyses of public opinion in the Federal Republic of Germany and in the German Democratic Republic, and on a cross-sectional analysis of West German attitudes. Much of the public opinion data is published here for the first time; the book as a whole presents a unique collection of public opinion polls on the German Question.

ISBN 0 8039 9932 1 **Cloth £5.00**
ISBN 0 8039 9931 3 **Paper £3.00** **March 1975**

LATIN AMERICA, THE COLD WAR AND THE WORLD POWERS, 1945-1973; A study in diplomatic history

F. Parkinson **Volume 9**

Most works dealing with Latin America's foreign policy have tended to focus on the area's relationship with the United States and have viewed this relationship from an American rather than a Latin American perspective. With the new prominence of the underdeveloped areas in world affairs and that of Latin America in particular, there has been a growing need to correct this imbalance. This book is the first systematic attempt to do so by concentrating on the foreign policies of Latin America toward world powers since 1945. Indeed, this work merits the attention of all interested in Latin America.

ISBN 0 8039 0413 4 **Cloth £5.00**
ISBN 0 8039 0412 6 **Paper £3.00** **December 1974**

MODELLING AND MANAGING INTERNATIONAL CONFLICTS: The Berlin Crisis

Volume 6

Raymond Tanter

Offers a variety of explanations for variations and levels of intensity in East-West conflicts. Raymond Tanter proposes a method for the general modelling of international conflict and more accurate prediction of the actors' choices in such situations and goes on to suggest applications to conflict management in other international crises.

ISBN 0 8039 0330 8 **Cloth £5.00**
ISBN 0 8039 0329 4 **Paper £3.00** **December 1974**

SAGE Publications Ltd
44 Hatton Garden
London EC1N 8ER
Telephone: 01-242 7723

SAGE Publications Inc.
275 South Beverly Drive
Beverly Hills, California 90212
Telephone: (213) 274-8003

Police power, police practices:
the development of a 20th Century phenomenon

POLICE FORCES IN HISTORY

Editor George L. Mosse *University of Wisconsin at Madison*

Fifteen international articles which deal with police forces and agents in significant modern contexts – their role and their effect in some critical places and periods.

CONTENTS

February 1975	*333pp*	*Cloth £5.00*	*ISBN 8039 9934 8*
		Paper £2.50	*ISBN 8039 9928 3*

SAGE Publications Ltd
44 Hatton Garden London EC1N 8ER 01-242 7723